Ghosts

OF THE REVOLUTIONARY WAR

CHRISTOPHER E. WOLF

4880 Lower Valley Road, Atglen, Pennsylvania 19310

Disclaimer and Acknowledgment of Trademarks

All views are expressed by individuals and are not meant to be associated with any official National Park Service facility or historic site. This book is derived from the author's independent research.

Schiffer Books are available at special discounts for bulk purchases for sales promotions or premiums. Special editions, including personalized covers, corporate imprints, and excerpts can be created in large quantities for special needs. For more information contact the publisher:

Schiffer Publishing Ltd.
4880 Lower Valley Road
Atglen, PA 19310
Phone: (610) 593-1777; Fax: (610) 593-2002
E-mail: Info@schifferbooks.com

For the largest selection of fine reference books on this and related subjects, please visit our web site at
www.schifferbooks.com
We are always looking for people to write books on new and related subjects. If you have an idea for a book please contact us at the above address.

This book may be purchased from the publisher. Include $5.00 for shipping. Please try your bookstore first. You may write for a free catalog.

In Europe, Schiffer books are distributed by
Bushwood Books
6 Marksbury Ave.
Kew Gardens
Surrey TW9 4JF England
Phone: 44 (0) 20 8392-8585; Fax: 44 (0) 20 8392-9876
E-mail: info@bushwoodbooks.co.uk
Website: www.bushwoodbooks.co.uk

Designed by Stephanie Daugherty
Type set in Edwardian Script ITC/Engravers/New Baskerville BT
ISBN: 978-0-7643-3494-8
Printed in The United States of America

Dedication

This book is dedicated to my wonderful wife, Cindy. She has been not only a great help to me in creating this book, but her photography skills have made it better than I could hope for.

Courtesy of Cindy Wolf

Acknowledgments

I t takes a lot of helpful people to write a book such as the one you're now holding in your hands. I would like to thank everyone involved in making this project happen. If I've missed your name, it's not intentional; please bear with me. I'd first like to thank my editor at Schiffer Publishing, Dinah Roseberry, for going to bat for me to get this project approved for publication.

I'd also like to give credit to a public institution that was very helpful in creating this book, The Public Library System. Folks, if you're reading this, please support your local free public library; it's a valuable resource for everyone and right now many of the libraries are in danger of losing government funding.

I'd like to extend a thank you to all the National Park Service personnel – you do a great job of maintaining our country's historical sites.

Finally, I'd like to take this opportunity to again thank my wife, Cindy, for supplying me with another batch of great photographs for this book.

Courtesy of Christopher E. Wolf

Contents

Introduction

The Revolutionary War was a volatile time in our country's history. It was also a time of wonder and invention. From the years 1775 to 1781, the War of Independence raged across all thirteen colonies. During this time of upheaval, men like John Adams, Ben Franklin, John Hancock, and of course, the "Father" of our country, George Washington, went on to become larger than life historical legends.

I've always loved ghost stories and everywhere my wife and I travel (and we travel quite a bit), I like to collect books on local ghost lore and find no embarrassment asking a local resident if they know of any local hauntings.

I'm also a history buff and I have a great interest in the Civil War. Part of that interest comes from my love of a good ghost story and there have been literally hundreds of books and articles written about Civil War hauntings in general, and more specifically, Gettysburg, Pennsylvania. I always liked getting my history lesson with a dose of the supernatural mixed in.

Revolutionary War re-enactors getting into the Spirit of 76'. *Courtesy of Christopher E. Wolf*

In all my travels there was one type of book that I haven't been able to find: a book exclusively about Revolutionary War era hauntings. My first book, *Ghosts of Hershey and Vicinity*, was written because I couldn't find any books on hauntings in the Hershey, Pennsylvania area. This book has been written for the same reason. Now, I don't claim to be the first person to have ever written about a Revolutionary War haunting, but to the best of my knowledge, I'm the first person to write a book exclusively focusing on Revolutionary War spirits of the original thirteen colonies...and I hope to write several more of them.

But, what exactly are we talking about here? What kinds of hauntings and spirits can you expect to read about in this book? First, let's take a general look at different types of spirits and ghosts; then I'll explain what is meant by a Revolutionary War spirit and how I chose what hauntings to use in this book.

What do I mean when I say the word ghost? Webster's New World Dictionary lists a ghost as:

"The supposed disembodied spirit of a dead person, appearing as a pale, shadowy apparition."

It's a good description of a typical ghost, but it hardly scratches the surface of paranormal research. There are several types of ghosts and hauntings, such as poltergeists, shadow people, residual hauntings, and intelligent hauntings, just to name a few. I'll try to give you some examples of the most common types of hauntings and explain in more detail what they are. I'll start with one of the most common hauntings: The Residual Haunting.

THE RESIDUAL HAUNTING

A Residual Haunting is one that replays itself over and over again. Its very much like a video recording that is stuck in a loop. Most of the time the spirit or spirits are unaware that they are dead and are being witnessed by the living. As far as the haunting is concerned, the entities involved aren't aware of anything but their own situation in their own time period.

A Residual Haunting is rarely frightening, although if you're taken by surprise it can be startling, and if the scene depicted in the haunting is a nasty or violent death, you might be justified to be frightened. One positive side to this type of haunting is that it is not often physically harmful. A good example of a Revolutionary War

The Hessians are coming! The Hessians are coming! *Courtesy of Christopher E. Wolf*

residual haunting would be a scene of spectral soldiers re-enacting the Battle of Brandywine in Pennsylvania.

POLTERGEIST

Another type of haunting is a Poltergeist haunting. Some paranormal researchers think that a Poltergeist is the unconscious emotional energy that has been suppressed by either a pre-teen or teenager manifesting itself subconsciously affecting the surrounding area by making knocking sounds and moving objects. Usually the entity only acts up when the person creating it is nearby. Another theory is that since some teens are so emotionally charged, they might be able to subconsciously feed an entity and allow it to manifest itself.

A good example might be the Indian Shutters Restaurant. There might be a Revolutionary War spirit trapped in the restaurant and a member of the staff or someone who lives nearby might be the source of its energy.

THE INTELLIGENT HAUNTING

A third type of spirit would be what we call an Intelligent Haunting. Not that this means the ghost is super smart; it just means that it has the capacity to think for itself and to interact with the living to some degree. This type of ghost sometimes knows that it has passed on in life, but is still linked to this earthly realm. The spirit may be confused or disoriented, but it will attempt to communicate with the living, by either speaking in a disembodied voice or fully manifesting and appearing as a live person. Not all Intelligent Hauntings are the same. In fact, most Intelligent Hauntings are unique.

A good example of an Intelligent Haunting would be the Deacon's ghost I encountered in the Old Dutch Burying Ground in Sleepy Hollow several years ago.

***

Most paranormal researchers agree that a place is usually haunted because of a large outpouring of emotion happened there. Consequently, many Revolutionary War battlefields, such as The Brandywine Battlefield in Pennsylvania and Yorktown in Williamsburg, Virginia, have a lot of paranormal sightings. There are numerous hauntings that have occurred and are still occurring today throughout the states that began as the original thirteen Colonies. From the cold New England colony of New Hampshire's Indian Shutters Restaurant, through the hills and streams of Valley Forge in the Middle Colony of Pennsylvania, to the Southern Colony in Georgia at the tragic scene of Mackay's Trading House, one thing is certainly clear: Old patriots never die...and they refuse to just fade away.

Section One:

HAUNTINGS

IN THE

NEW ENGLAND

COLONIES

The provinces of New Hampshire, Massachusetts Bay, Rhode Island and the Providence Plantations, and lastly, Connecticut are the New England colonies. They have a long and rich history dating back to the Pilgrims who settled in 1620 and the Puritans who followed shortly in 1629. It is not surprising that they also have a long and colorful haunted history as well.

Strangely enough, England was not really trying to colonize New England in any sort of organized manner. Most early English colonists had gone there for their own reasons, independent of the government. For example: The Pilgrims and the Puritans went to New England in hopes of gaining religious freedom.

Other groups left Europe because of the overcrowding in many European cities. There were those, too, that saw America as an opportunity to create a vast amount of money. But, by far, the largest group of colonists weren't even sure they wanted to be there in the first place. Over fifty percent of the early colonists in New England were sent there as either convicts or as indentured servants.

From its early days as a land of religious freedom, New England quickly grew into an area known for farming, trade, and a very prosperous shipbuilding center of America. New England has a long and colorful paranormal history encompassing the witches of Salem, Massachusetts, to the dealings with the devil in New Hampshire and in the haunted battlefields around Lexington. The New England colonies have plenty of ghostly venues well worth a visit, and not only on a dark and stormy night.

The Province of
New Hampshire

"Live Free or Die: Death is not the worst of evils."

~General John Stark
New Hampshire's most famous soldier of the Revolutionary War

The Province of New Hampshire has had many firsts in a long history. It was the first post-colonial sovereign nation in America. It's one of the first original thirteen colonies. It was also one of the first provinces to strike a blow in the Revolutionary War against England. With all these firsts, I felt that New Hampshire should have the honor of being the first chapter in this book of ghostly Revolutionary War tales.

New Hampshire was named after the county of Hampshire, England. Even though New Hampshire was one of the first Provinces to declare independence from England, only one really significant Revolutionary War action took place in there. The Raid on Fort William and Mary took place on the night of December 14, 1774 – two years before the signing of the Declaration of Independence.

Even then, New Hampshirites were ahead of everybody else in the colonies. Thanks to some timely espionage work by none other than Paul Revere – (yes, the same Paul Revere so well known for the *one if by land two if by sea* fame) – he'd warned the budding Sons of Liberty, who were planning on raiding the Fort William and Mary, the night of December 13th, that the Fort was reinforced by troops from Boston. Armed with this knowledge,

The guns are silent now, but during the Revolutionary War, they sounded the call to freedom. *Courtesy of Cindy Wolf*

the Patriots were able to storm the fort and capture it from the British commander without any bloodshed from either side. Not a bad night's work! According to reports, the raid lasted for two nights. The first night of the raid was carried out by local Patriots living in the nearby town of Portsmouth.

On the second night of the raid, General Sullivan of the newly formed Continental Army took command. General Sullivan is credited with having fired the first shot in the Revolutionary War. Sullivan described what they had captured in the raid as: remains of gunpowder, small firearms, bayonets, cartuche boxes together with cannons and ordinance – a good haul for the two-night raid. The gunpowder was hidden in the house of Major Demerit, a patriot living in Portsmouth. Eventually, the powder and cannons were distributed among the various Continental Army units during the Revolutionary War. There are even those who claim that some of the cannons and powder were used at the Battle of Bunker Hill. But, no one can prove or disprove this. One thing that is for certain: New Hampshire has no lack of haunted places that date back to the Revolutionary War.

General Jonathan Moulton
Marriage Problems and the Devil

General Jonathan Moulton has become an important figure in not only New Hampshire history, but in the Revolutionary War and the founding of the United States itself.

He was born in Hampton, New Hampshire, on July 2, 1721. As a youth, he was apprenticed to a cabinetmaker, a vocation that was clearly not suited to him at all. In 1745, at the age of 24, he was appointed the rank of captain in the Rangers of the New Hampshire Militia. It was to be the start of a long and exemplary military career.

As a young Captain, Jonathan Moulton saw his share of action when the New Hampshire Militia, as part of the New England army under the command of William Peppermill, he helped secure Fort Louisbourg from the French. For the next three years, he spent fighting the Ossippee Indians during the war known as King Phillip's War.

As a reward for his outstanding service, Moulton was granted large tracts of land. These were on the north side of Lake Winneppesaukee, and included the towns of New Harrington, Tamworth, Center Harbor, Sandwich, and last of all, Moultonborough, which he named after himself. Jonathan Moulton married his childhood sweetheart, Abigail Smith in 1749. They would go on to have and raise eleven children over the next twenty years. Evidently, he was what we would now call a workaholic. (He almost had to be to support a family of thirteen!)

Alongside his farm and mansion, he owned and ran a general store that sold, among other things, Braziery, cutlery ware, and almost everything suitable for housekeeping. He was also a representative of the New England Legislature and a financial opportunist of the first order. The latter not making him very popular with his neighbors and leading to the first of many legends about the man who was to become known as the "Yankee Faust."

In the wee hours of the morning of March 15th, 1769, Moulton's magnificent mansion, with its furniture imported from across the sea from England, was burned to the ground. He eventually built another modest home and it was known to be the finest house in New Hampshire prior to the Revolution. But what he couldn't rebuild so readily with his vast fortune was his personal reputation. Jonathan Moulton was never well liked as a person, and this dislike may have contributed to the flash fire of rumors that soon flamed into bona fide legend about the man. Speaking of fire, it's this basic element of nature that plays a major role in one of the most well-known legends about General Moulton.

Jonathan Moulton was by all accounts a wealthy man even before the Revolutionary War. Tales of his greed were often gossiped around the taverns of New Hampshire. Granted people may have been jealous of his wealth; there must have been some truth to the rumors to begin with. But what could he have done that was so bad that it caused a major legend to spring up about the man? It was none other than Moulton making a deal with the devil himself!

The Legend goes like this: General Jonathan Moulton was a very greedy man. As rich and wealthy as he already was, he desired more and more gold. The story goes on to reveal that he made a deal with Satan in the manner of Dr. Faust by saying that he would sell his soul to the devil if the devil would agree to fill up his boots with gold coins on the first day of every month until the day he died.

Having made the statement, suddenly flames arose in the fireplace and out stepped a man with a pointy beard wearing a burnt charcoal suit.

"Just prick thy finger on the quill and sign your name at the bottom and we have a deal," said the devil, holding out a piece of parchment towards the General.

His greed outranked his fear and Jonathan Moulton bled into the quill pen and signed his soul over to the devil. Bowing deeply, the devil stepped back into the roaring flames in the hearth, smiled with pointy teeth and said to Moulton, "A pleasure doing business with you my good sir!" Then he vanished in a cloud of smoke and brimstone.

Quickly regaining his wits about him, Moulton found and bought the largest pair of boots in all the Province of New Hampshire. They were reputed to be so big that when they were hung from the mantle of the fireplace they actually touched the floor.

The next month as agreed, the devil returned to fill the boots with gold coins. As the devil poured handful after handful of coins into the boots, they never seemed to fill up! You see, Jonathan Moulton, not content to acquire a pair of boots full of gold each month, had cut out the soles of the boots and placed them over a hole in the floor, so that all of the gold coins would fall through to the basement of the house.

The Devil, having not been born only yesterday and he himself being the father of all deceit, quickly saw through Moulton's trick and in a fit of rage burnt down the fine mansion to the ground. When the house was extinguished, much to Jonathan's dismay, no gold was ever found. This is, after all, a book of ghost stories and after his house was modestly rebuilt on the same spot, it was this new house that acquired the reputation for being haunted.

The most famous haunting of Moulton happened at the start of the Revolutionary War. On the eve of the revolution, Jonathan Moulton made the choice to fight on the side of the Patriots. Shortly after being commissioned as a colonel of the 3rd Regiment of the New Hampshire Militia, tragedy struck the Moulton household.

Abigail Moulton, Jonathan's wife of twenty years and mother of his eleven children, was struck down and killed by smallpox and was buried in the garden outside of the house. I'm sure Jonathan Moulton took time to grieve, but it seems as though he moved on with his life rather quickly.

Less than a year after Abigail's death, he married a younger woman by the name of Sarah Emery, the widow of a man killed at the Battle of Concord. Despite having four more children, the marriage was off to a rocky start.

As the new bride retired for the night she discovered several pieces of jewelry in her dresser drawer including a necklace and a ring that belonged to Abigail Moulton. Jonathan explained that yes, they belonged to his deceased wife, but that he was sure she would want her to have them. He placed Abigail's ring on Sarah's finger himself.

Jonathan may have been a competent, if not great military man, but he had a lot to learn about women – a lesson he was about to learn. They both settled into bed, but sleep was not to come easily for Sarah. She was already uneasy about having become so quickly the newest Mrs. Moulton. Repeatedly throughout the darkening evening she had the distinct feeling that there was somebody watching her from the shadows throughout the house. She climbed into bed next to the already sleeping Jonathan and was finally able to rest after her busy and exhausting wedding day.

No sooner had she closed her weary eyes when she heard a faint voice moan, "Miiiiiiiinnnnneeee! Miiinee! Miinnee!" It sounded as though it were coming from the window. She slowly roused herself out of bed and cautiously crept over to the window as the faint moonlight created unfamiliar shadows across the floor. She gazed out the window at the full moon. "Mine! Mine! Miiiinnneee!" wailed a voice directly behind her. Sarah spun around and instantly was face to face with the spectral face of Abigail, the deceased Mrs. Moulton! The sight of the dead woman was too much for Sarah. She screamed and then fainted on the spot.

Her cry of fright awakened Jonathan and most of the rest of the household. Once everyone settled back down and Sarah regained consciousness, they noticed that her hand was bloody and scratched and the finger she had worn Abigail's ring on was...empty!

The ring belonging to Abigail was gone! Jonathan took one look at his new wife's hand and went white as a sheet.

The next day before leaving to command his troops in the Revolution, he had the body of Abigail disinterred from her resting place in the garden. When the twelve-month-old coffin was opened, a shock awaited the observers.

Abigail's body was still somewhat intact, but what drew all their attention was the shiny ring on her skeletal finger. The ring that until the previous night had adorned Sarah's finger! Jonathan Moulton was so shaken by the sight that he immediately had the coffin resealed and reburied without a headstone.

This tale was told so often that it eventually became a popular folktale in New Hampshire and the rest of New England. The famous poet J.G. Whittier wrote a ballad called, "The New Wife and the Old" which helped perpetuate the story for future generations of ghost story lovers.

General Jonathan Moulton went on to lead his troops at the second battle of Saratoga in 1777. After the Revolutionary War ended, he lost some of his wealth in the post-war depression and on September 18, 1787, he died suddenly and was laid to rest next to his first wife, Abigail, in the garden outside his home. Strangely enough, there was no headstone to mark his resting place, and since he had removed Abigail's headstone years earlier, no one to this day is really sure where Jonathan Moulton or Abigail Moulton is buried on the property.

After Moulton's death, the house had gained the nickname: "The Haunted House." Over the years, an apparition of a large black hound has been known to appear and disappear on the property. The dog isn't the only apparition. For whatever reason, the sound of a large grandfather clock will strike and then the sound will disappear only to reappear to strike again later. No one has been able to find this elusive clock in the house.

Slaves who lived and worked in the house claimed to have seen ghosts and later owners of the house, the Whipples, believed it was it was haunted and had witnessed enough paranormal activity to have the house exorcised by the church. Nobody knows which church did the exorcism, but it is definitely on record that the ritual took place in the early twentieth century.

Years later, after Jonathan had passed away, Sarah Moulton was asked by a reporter if the legends were true about her deceased husband. The second Mrs. Moulton replied by saying that she really couldn't deny the truth to the rumors that had circulated about her late husband, the General.

Haunts of the
Indian Shutters Restaurant

In the southwestern corner of the state of New Hampshire, sometimes known as the "Quiet Corner," sits the cozy, pleasant town of Charlestown. But it was not always so quiet. Early in its history the little village that would become Charlestown was know as Plantation No. 4 and was the first place attacked by French Troops and Native Americans intent on forcing the British colonists to flee the area. What they did instead was to rally their forces and create a fortified village known as Fort No. 4. Through the efforts of Captain Phineas Stevens and his brave band of Militia the superior numbers of the French and Native American forces were repelled after a brutal siege and the British Colonials managed to retain ownership of the land.

Several years later, the tale of how Captain Stevens and his militia had saved the day reached the ears of Sir Charles Knowles, a British Admiral who was living in Boston. Sir Charles was so impressed with what he had heard about Fort No. 4 and Captain Stevens that he sent his sword as a token of gratitude for their courage and sacrifice.

The people of the town were so awed with the gesture that they returned one of their own: They renamed the town Charlestown in the Admiral's honor and from that time forward Fort No. 4 was known as Charlestown.

But the people of Charlestown had only just begun to experience the turmoil of war. As the Revolutionary War swept across the country, Charlestown had become a supply depot and recruitment town for the Continental Army.

Charlestown has many homes and buildings that date back to the 1700s. Charlestown's Main Street is one of the longest listed National Register of Historic Homes. It's also home to a few hardy colonial spirits as well.

Today, the Indian Shutters Restaurant is known for its fine food, but it was once known as the Parker Tavern. Along with its cheerful dining room atmosphere and cozy lower level pub you might run into a spirit or two...or three.

The Parker family was one of the first settlers in the Charlestown area, dating back when it was known as Plantation No. 4 and then Fort No. 4. A prominent member of the Parkers was a man named Isaac Parker. He was a Lieutenant in the local Militia under several different Captains. In 1746, he and two other men, Captain John Spafford and Stephen Farnsworth, were the first to be taken captive by the Indians attacking Fort No. 4. They were released the following winter under a flag of truce.

Ten years later in 1756, Lieutenant Parker was put in command of Fort No. 4 when its previous commander, Captain Phineas Stevens left to continue fighting the war in Nova Scotia.

During his lifetime, Isaac Parker proved to be a shrewd businessman in Charlestown and held the confidence of his fellow townsfolk as a duly elected Selectman and Moderator up until his death on April Fools Day, 1762.

It's this family of colonists that owned the Parker Tavern that is now known as the Indian Shutters Restaurant. As hauntings go, the Indian Shutters has its share of apparitions throughout the building.

Both the staff and patrons of the establishment have seen and heard the spirit known as General Parker. General Parker is believed to be the spirit of a Revolutionary War general that once owned and lived in the building. He's been spotted in the current owner's living quarters and may also be the shadowy figure haunting the downstairs storage room. Not much is known about the general. In fact, he may not have even been a general.

My research into the Parker family doesn't show any of them holding the rank of general during, before, or after the Revolutionary War. Regardless of what rank the ghost held during the war, it holds the rank of the most active spirit in the restaurant.

Another colonial-era spirit makes her presence known to customers and staff alike by appearing in various mirrors placed throughout the dining room. This female spirit appears dressed in a white colonial-style dress and is very frequently spotted looking out of the large set of mirrors directly behind the buffet table.

Guests who make their way downstairs to the newly built bar have felt extreme coldness as they walk along a very old stone-walled hallway. It's at the end of this hall, in a storage room, that employees have spotted a shadowy figure moving about the dark recesses of the room between storage racks. Nobody has ever gotten a good look at the figure but, some people feel he's either the general or another colonial-era spirit making his presence known. So be aware, if you plan on going to the Indian Shutters for some fine food and spirits, you might just encounter some spirits of a different sort.

The Massachusetts Bay Colony and Maine

By the rude bridge that arched the flood,
Their flag to April's breeze unfurled;
Here once the embattled farmers stood,
And fired the shot heard 'round the world.

~Ralph Waldo Emerson's Concord Hymn,
describing the impact that the battle
at the Old North Bridge in Concord, Massachusetts,
had during the beginning of the Revolutionary War
on April 19, 1775

The name *Massachusetts* comes from the name of a Native American tribe that lived in the area. Translated into English it means: *The people who live near the great hill.*

The Massachusetts Bay colony was first chartered on October 7th 1691, by William and Mary, the joint rulers of England and Scotland – even though the Pilgrims had landed on Plymouth Rock in November of 1620. It's because of the hard work and sacrifice of those early Pilgrims seeking religious freedom that we get to have a feast on Thanksgiving every year. This is the simplified version that all school children are taught in school and most people think that this was all it took to start the Massachusetts Bay colony. The real story is much more interesting and even more subject to debate.

To say that Massachusetts was a social and religious powder keg would be like saying the American Civil War was a family squabble.

Consider this: One major group of colonists comprised the Puritans, a loose collection of people with some similar religious beliefs, the main conviction being that the Church of England was corrupt and that they themselves were being persecuted by the church. The other large group was comprised of convicts or people who had been forced to go to the colonies against their will as indentured servants.

The first thing the Puritans did when they arrived in Massachusetts was to enforce their beliefs on everyone else whether they were Puritan or non-Puritan. Since most of the Puritans were in local positions of power, it was fairly easy for them to do this.

This persecution manifested itself at its peak at the Salem Witch Trials. During those dark days, no less than nineteen men and women were executed as witches. Family pets weren't even safe – they even executed two dogs as witch's familiars. Hundreds of other Non-Puritan conformists were imprisoned as well.

Not to be outclassed by Salem, Plymouth also held witchcraft trials, but fortunately, no one was executed. Once the fury died down, wiser heads prevailed and the witch trials were condemned and most of the people involved were punished or at least forced to make a public apology. Massachusetts remained a colony until October 7th, 1774, when the General Court of Massachusetts established the Massachusetts Provincial Congress as a prelude to revolting in the American Revolutionary War.

Seven months later at The Battle of Concord, the famous "Shot Heard 'Round the World" would officially start the battle for American independence from England. It's easy to see why Massachusetts has such patriotic and haunted heritage.

The Ghostly Prophet of Hilton Neck

Young Nellie Hilton had always marched to the beat of her own drum. She loved the outdoors and would today be considered a tomboy. Back in the Mid-1700s of Puritan-governed Plymouth, Massachusetts, she was considered at best a huge problem child for her father and the other townsfolk. Besides being a willful outspoken child, even more of a problem for her family was that she despised the strict constraints put upon her by the Puritan lifestyle. She was headstrong, independent, and refused to obey the strict Puritan social guidelines laid down by the town elders.

Finally, her poor father could take no more of his daughter's anti-social behavior, and to the delight of Nell, moved the family to Jonesboro, Maine, in 1740. There, the Puritans had less of an influence on society and Nell had plenty of open, outdoor spaces to explore for her curiosity.

Always an outdoors and wilderness soul, Nell naturally made friends with the neighboring native American Indians. The closet tribe to her home was the Passamaquoddy tribe, and as young Nell grew into womanhood, she fell in love with one of the local Indian braves.

Their love was strong and the honorable brave was going to take Nell for his bride. But poor Nell never had the chance at happiness for very long. Having kept her lover for a secret for so long, it was inevitable that her father would find out about the tryst and so he did in the most awful and gut-wrenching way possible.

He happened accidentally upon Nell and her brave in the throes of passionate lovemaking. Mr. Hilton, enraged beyond rational thought, grabbed the first weapon that he could find, a hatchet, and killed and scalped the poor unsuspecting brave right in front of his own terrified daughter.

After calming down and sending the Brave's lifeless body back to the tribe for a proper burial ritual, her father demanded Nell to tell him how such an act could have taken place under his roof. He thought that the brave had attacked and raped her against her will.

Nell, being the willful and honest woman that she was tearfully told her father that the man he had killed was in fact her betrothed and even produced a wedding ring to prove it to him.

Her father insisted that she find a suitable mate from among her own people and demanded she start acting like a woman of proper society.

Nell, obstinate to the last bit of her heart, refused and so in another fit of rage her father yelled, "If you love the red man so much then, abandon this house at go out in the woods and live among the savages!"

Nell did just that. She gathered her belongings, left her father's house that very night, and for the next thirty-five years of her life, Nell lived among the various native tribes in Maine and Canada.

Nell was ahead of her time, not to mention a progressive woman, not just in her own century, but she would've been considered a role model for women even in the twentieth century. She was a negotiator and translator to the French Canadians and the native Americans; it was rumored that she also worked as a schoolteacher in Brunswick and areas of Maine.

But Nell Hilton had yet to show her most special talent – a talent that some people would consider a gift and others might consider a curse.

In 1755, she made a reappearance in her old hometown of Jonesboro, Maine, the scene of her life-changing tragedy with her father. She had a message for the townsfolk: A war was coming. Amazingly, she foretold about the French and Indian War. Not only about how it would start, but also how it would end. She was correct in all accounts as to what was to happen.

Strangely, after making her prophecy, she returned to the wilderness and no one knew where she'd gone for twenty years until 1775, when she again mysteriously returned to Jonesboro to make another, even more amazing prophecy. Nell predicted the coming Revolutionary War.

This wasn't big news to most people of the time. Rumors of war had been brooding around the local taverns. Most people believed that war was inevitable and they took her prediction with a grain of salt.

But where Nell's prophecy differed from other war speculations was in the fact that she accurately predicted the very first engagement of the war at the Battle of Lexington and went on to predict that the Patriots would ultimately win the war and that the British would surrender at Yorktown.

Nell was imprisoned by the British as a spy shortly after her appearance in Jonesboro. They felt that she had collaborated with the French and the Native Americans during the French and Indian wars and now felt that she was aiding the Continental Army against them as well.

They took her into custody and on March 1st, 1777, she was hung as a spy at the gallows of St. John, New Brunswick. But before she died, as defiant as ever, while standing on the gallows plank with the noose around her neck, she made an oath to all who would be listening that day.

Nell Hilton vowed that her spirit would return on the anniversary of her death at a spot now known as "Prophecy Rock" whenever war threatened American soil.

So, has Nell kept her vow? Some people think so. Her spirit has been sighted several times in the past right before a war. Nell's ghost has been seen before the War of 1812, the Mexican War in 1846, the American Civil War in 1861, the Spanish-American War in 1898, and just before World War I. Since then, no one has reported seeing her spirit. That's not to say she hasn't kept her promise and made an appearance. It just may mean that no one has been looking for her.

The Witch's Curse

On the outskirts of a very old seaport town called Bucksport, on the Penopscot Bay, there's a small, wrought iron enclosed family cemetery plot. Inside is the final resting place of the Buck family, some of the first settlers of the town. Inside is also a ghostly legend.

Bucksport, Maine, was named after the highly respected yet infamous, Colonel Jonathan Buck. Not only does Bucksport have one ripping good ghost story, it also has good physical evidence to support the ghostly tale.

You'll want – no let me rephrase that – you'll have to take a leisurely drive along the windy, craggy coast of Maine, passing through several quaint New England towns, to reach the town of Bucksport. Perched on the Northern end of Penopscot Bay, the little town harbors the cursed tomb of its namesake and one of its founders: Colonel Jonathan Buck.

Jonathan Buck was born in 1719, in the town of Woburn, Massachusetts. Before becoming commissioned as a Colonel by the General Court of Massachusetts, Jonathan Buck led the fairly mundane life of a land surveyor and shipbuilder in Haverhill, Massachusetts with his father.

He was part of a sixty-man surveying expedition into the Penopscot Bay area of Maine in 1762. It was this expedition that led him to help start a settlement two years later that would eventually be known as the town of Bucksport.

By all accounts, Colonel Buck was a very intense man with strong convictions and "dark, penetrating eyes." Buck was always resentful of the way the British ruled the colonies and had always been outspoken against the injustices done to them by the crown.

As the Revolutionary War began, Colonel Buck became one of the outstanding patriots in an area that was largely loyal to the crown. Jonathan Buck raised his own troops, the 5th militia, and proceeded to help take part in the storming of the British at Castine and the Siege at Fort George in July of 1779. The twenty-one day battle turned out to be an unmitigated defeat for the rebels. In fact, until Pearl Harbor, it was considered the largest American Naval defeat in history.

The very next day, after the Patriots retreated from the British, Colonel Buck, at the age of 60, and suffering from gout, walked 200 miles from Bucksport to Haverhill, Massachusetts in order to escort his wife, and his daughter, Lydia, who was seriously ill at the time, to safety.

Meanwhile, the Redcoats were busy pillaging and burning all the property belonging to the rebels in the Penopscot Bay settlements, including Jonathan Buck's homestead. Colonel Buck sent his family to Brewer for safety before moving on to Haverhill.

After the Revolutionary War ended, Jonathan Buck and his family returned to the Penopscot Bay area to rebuild his old homestead and to make a fresh start. So where does the ghost story come in to play? I'm glad you asked. There are several different versions of why Colonel Buck's tomb is cursed and haunted by a witch's footprint.

VERSION ONE

The most popular version of the legend is immortalized in a poem called, "The Foot of Tucksport" by Robert P. Tristam Coffin. It was a very blatant reference to Bucksport and Colonel Buck's tombstone.

In the Poem, the main character is Colonel Jonathan Jethro Tuck and he's been accused of fathering a boy out of wedlock with an accused witch. She confronts him in the town square and the outraged townspeople drag her away:

> *They dragged the crone to her poor hut*
> *They tied her to the door,*
> *They brought and heaped the withered boughs,*
> *Against the rags she wore.*
>
> *The thunderhead touched on the sun,*
> *And a shadow came,*
> *Just as Colonel Tuck bent down*
> *And touched the boughs with flame.*

Okay, so it sounds like Colonel Tuck (or Buck) sent a witch to burn at the stake. Right? But, consider this: At the time Jonathan Buck was born, the Salem Witch Trials had been over for more than thirty years. Furthermore, no accused witch was ever actually burned at the stake in New England. Most of them were hung. There's no record of any official witch trials in Maine, and even if there were, Jonathan Buck was only a Justice of the Peace. He didn't have the authority to hold a trial any more than anyone else who lived in Bucksport.

At the end of Coffin's poem, the dying witch curses Colonel Tuck:

> *"And so long as a monument*
> *Marks a grave of thine*
> *So long shall my curse inscribe*
> *Thy tombstone with my sign!"*

Colonel Jonathan Buck died on March 18, 1795, at 4:30 p.m. and was buried in a little family cemetery a short distance east of Bucksport. At first, there was only a small grave marker, but in 1852, a fifteen-foot-tall granite obelisk monument was erected in his honor by his descendants. It is this monument that is the centerpiece of the cursed legend. On one side is an inscription that reads:

Col. Jonathan Buck
The Founder of Bucksport
A.D. 1762
Born in Haverhill, Mass. 1719
Died March 18, 1795

On the front of the Obelisk there is simply inscribed the name: BUCK. It's what's underneath this inscription that has caused all the controversy. Shortly after the monument was erected, there appeared to be a blemish in the granite that has the shape of a booted, or in some people's opinion, a female foot and leg stomping or dancing above the grave.

It is well documented that the relatives had chosen an exceptionally, clean and unblemished piece of granite. So where did the stain come from? Some people assumed it was the work of disrespectful vandals and they attempted to have the granite cleaned with a solution, but despite their attempts the stain remained visible.

In fact, because of their attempts, it became even more prominent. Allegedly, they tried to gouge out the imperfection, but it resisted removal. Supposedly, the monument has been replaced three times and each time the image of the foot returns.

The legend of the cursed tomb has grown over the centuries. Another version of the legend claims that curse was called down on Colonel Buck, not by the witch herself, but by her deformed son:

> *" Your Tomb shall thee bear the mark of a witch's foot, for all eternity!"*

Is this the proof of a witch's curse?

VERSION TWO

Yet another version of the legend has nothing to do with witchcraft. It takes place in either Massachusetts or Maine and involves the finding of the grisly remains of a woman. One of her legs had been sawn off at the time of the discovery.

Because of the public pressure of finding the murderer quickly, "Judge" Buck had a mentally impaired hermit who lived in crude shack at the edge of town, brought in as the main suspect. In what was probably best described as a kangaroo court, the poor hermit was quickly pronounced guilty of the crime and sentenced to death. On his way to his execution, he looked at Buck and swore that he was innocent and that his proof would be the image of the dead woman's leg on Buck's gravestone.

VERSION THREE

A third version, and this one might actually be closer to the truth than any of the previous ones, has a very different curse attached to the Buck family. A blogger on the Internet claims to be married to one of the descendants of Colonel Buck and their story differs quite a bit from popular legend.

The Buck family story goes that Colonel Buck had an affair with a young Native American woman and she became pregnant as the result. Not wanting his reputation to be ruined, he accused her of being a witch and had her burned at the stake to cover up his indiscretion. Now here's where the tale differs from the others.

The mother of the girl Colonel Buck had executed actually was a witch and cursed Colonel Buck and the entire Buck family. She vowed that they would never be rid of the girl's memory. The curse has manifested that every other generation of the Buck family line will have at least one child with strong Native American appearance.

The blogger claims that in this generation it's her mother-in-law and one of her sisters who have manifested the curse. To top it off, she writes that none of the children born in her husband's generation have those features. But, she and the rest of the family are waiting to see if the curse will effect this generation of the family.

***

In any case, no one can deny that there is something strange about the mark on Colonel Buck's Monument.

Curse or no curse? You can visit the tomb and see for yourself.

The Unlucky Lovers of The Session House

The Session House is located on the Campus of Smith College in Northampton, Massachusetts. It was built in 1700 by a man named John Hunt. Hunt built his house outside the walls of the nearby fort in Northampton. He knew this was dangerous for his family. Because of so many Indian attacks in the area, he built a secret escape passage that led to the nearby river in case of emergency. This tunnel, or passage if you will, played a major role in the haunting tale of tragedy associated with the Session House. But it has also given the Session House a Halloween tradition as well.

During the Revolutionary War the house was still in the possession of the Hunt family. The Hunts were supporters of the rebels and it is for this reason that British General John "Gentleman Johnny" Burgoyne was captured and placed under house arrest as a prisoner of war there.

General Burgoyne was a flamboyant and impetuous officer. He was generally well liked by his men, but he was also vain to the extreme and had a reputation with being a *love em' and leave 'em* type with the ladies – a personality trait that had hampered his career in the British army more than once in the past.

Burgoyne's life had its share of great successes and great failures. Born in London in 1722, Burgoyne studied at Westminster School and then left and joined the British Army in 1740. Not thinking about the effect it would have on his career in the military, he eloped in 1743 with 11th Earl of Derby's daughter to France to avoid overwhelming debts he had accrued while in London.

Burgoyne returned to England in 1756 and rejoined the British Army where he participated in the Seven Years War. After serving in the army, he was elected to Parliament in 1761 where he continued his climb to success by, in 1772, demanding and spearheading an investigation of the East India Company. In that same year, he was promoted to Major General and was sent for duty to Boston, Massachusetts, to continue serving in the British Army.

As rebellion broke out in the colonies, he witnessed the Battle of Bunker Hill in 1775, although he was not a participant in it. He later returned to England to report what he had witnessed. A year later, in 1776, he was chosen as second in command to Sir Guy Carleton to invade New York from Canada. It started out as moderate success.

The British managed to capture Crown Point on Lake Champlain. But, this wasn't enough for General Burgoyne.

Disgusted with the lack of leadership of Sir Guy, Burgoyne returned to London and used his charisma and charm to persuade the King and Prime Minister to allow him to lead the invasion of New York from Canada.

They gave their approval, and in June of 1777, Burgoyne was in command of an army of 7,000 troops. He and his army reoccupied Crown Point and then a month later went on to capture Fort Ticonderoga. This is where his plans for invading New York started to slowly unravel.

Burgoyne's army of Redcoats was moving south towards New York as planned, but his allies, Colonel Barry St. Leger and General William Howe were having problems. Colonel St. Leger was stopped in the west by the Americans was unable to bring the support troops that Burgoyne needed to counter the rebel army.

In the south, General Howe never received the orders to send support troops north. He was under the impression that he was supposed to send troops to Philadelphia. As a consequence, Burgoyne's army, greatly outnumbered by the Continental Army, was forced to stop at Bemis Heights. Eventually, after two attempts to break away from the Americans, Burgoyne was forced to surrender to General Horatio Gates at Saratoga on October 17, 1777.

As a prisoner of war, he was taken to the Hunt household and placed under house arrest as a Prisoner of War. Supposedly, while awaiting parole back to England, he fell in love with Lucy Hunt. The legend goes that, Lucy's father, a staunch supporter of the patriot cause, refused to allow her to see the incarcerated Burgoyne and would have been furiously opposed to any relationship between the two of them.

As a result, the two lovers would meet secretly in the hidden passage to profess their love for each other. Some historians believe that "Gentleman Johnny" was just using the young girl as a means of escape from the house; others believe that he was just using her to pass the time. I prefer the romanticized version that he may have actually been in love with the woman.

After many months of their secret meetings, Burgoyne was paroled back to England. Before leaving, however, he promised to come back for Lucy Hunt as soon as he was able. He never did return for her or for any other reason. Lucy Hunt died heartbroken.

But, what of Burgoyne? After returning to England, he was highly criticized for his surrender at Saratoga. Unbeknownst to him, that was the turning point in the war for the Patriots. After seeing him defeated, the French government decided to give their full support to George Washington and the rebels. Support that would eventually end up turning the tide of war in favor of the Americans.

Crushed by this revelation, Burgoyne briefly tried to rebuild his political career, but had little following. In 1783, he gave up on politics and began to pursue his first love: play writing. He enjoyed some moderate success.

Burgoyne died on August 4, 1792, and was buried in Westminster Abby. His body may be buried in London, but his spirit and the spirit of Lucy Hunt are reputed to haunt the secret passage that lies under Session House together in the afterlife.

A ceremony in the Session House evolved over the years based on the legend of the ghostly lovers. Each Halloween, the female students of the Session House are instructed to search for the hidden passage. The catch is that they have only twenty minutes to find it and – they have to do it in complete darkness. If they succeed, it's considered a special honor.

Who knows, they might even chance across the spirits of the unlucky lovers engaged in a secret rendezvous in the hidden passage after all these years.

Is Paul Revere Haunting His Old Workshop?

" Listen my children, and you shall hear,
of the midnight ride of Paul Revere..."

~Henry Wadsworth Longfellow

No doubt everyone has heard of the famous Revolutionary War hero, Paul Revere, and his horseback race across the New England countryside shouting, "The British are coming! The British are coming!"

Paul Revere was not just a bell-ringing courier for George Washington's Continental Army; he was also a prominent businessman in his own right with his silversmith shop in Boston. The Boston home of Paul Revere is open to the public as a museum. I've not heard of any hauntings associated with that building but, then Paul Revere never spent his last days there. No, Paul Revere the businessman and craftsman left the city of Boston behind, and in 1801 at the advanced age (back then) of 65, and began his largest entrepreneurial venture: Revere Copperworks.

It's no wonder people have had ghostly encounters at the Revere Copperworks; many times when a person puts all their energy and hard work into building, a place they love, it's hard to let go. Paul Revere was no exception.

He first became familiar with the Village of Canton during the Revolutionary War in 1776. He was an advisor to the rebel leaders on the manufacturing and use of gunpowder. Fourteen miles from his home in Boston, was a powder mill in Canton, a location he was familiar with. As much as he was interested in the powder mill for the Revolution's gunpowder, he saw an even greater opportunity for himself in the water power of the Neponset River. This was where he wanted to build his copper rolling mill. Along with the copper mill, Paul Revere also bought the former miller's home that was built in 1717. Renaming it Canton Dale, he settled into live the good life in the country.

Paul Revere decided to put all of his life savings into the copper mill. It was a risky venture. He purchased the site mainly because of the close proximity to a source of water power. It cost him $65,000, and if the venture failed, he would most likely be ruined. Thanks to his friends in the government, he was given a loan of $10,000 and 19,000 tons of copper to start his business off on the right foot. It was a booming business – one that lasted into the early twentieth century.

According to an anonymous blogger on the Shadowlands website, Paul Revere still makes his presence known in his old Canton Copperworks by moving objects and opening and closing doors, and even opening and closing windows.

The Canton home that Revere lived in, Canton Dale was so dilapidated that it was torn down sometime in the twentieth century, but evidently his old shop was converted into rental housing at some point and the families that lived in the house also experienced the otherworldly antics of the old silversmith. During this period in time, most of them even grew used to his presence.

Sadly, the last remnants of Paul Revere's copper mill are slated for demolition. In May of 2008, the owners of the property filed a demolition request with the Town of Canton to destroy the final two buildings on the property and is planning on building an Industrial Subdivision that will obliterate the historic Revere Buildings.

As a ground-breaking industrialist in the nineteenth century, Paul Revere set the standards of a fledgling copper industry. Is it any wonder that the old patriot is still haunting his old shop?

The Colony of
Rhode Island and
Providence Plantations

Rhode Island was the smallest colony in the new world. At just over 1,200 square miles, it doesn't lack the presence of the supernatural or a Revolutionary War history.

The founder of Rhode Island, a clergyman by the name of Roger Williams, was driven from the Massachusetts Bay company because he voiced his opinion of religious freedom – something the puritans wanted for themselves, but were opposed to granting to anyone who disagreed with their narrow-minded beliefs. Talk about hypocrisy!

Roger Williams formed a settlement on Narragansett Bay and called the town Providence. Freedom of speech and religious tolerance were the tenets that the town was built on.

In 1776, Rhode Island declared its independence from England and joined the other colonies in formal rebellion.

The Spirits of
the Nathanael Greene Homestead

"I am determined to defend my rights and maintain my freedom or sell my life in the attempt."

~General Nathanael Greene

Located in Cumberland, Rhode Island, sits Spell Hall. It's also known as the Nathanael Greene Homestead. It was the home of Revolutionary War General Nathanael Greene from 1770 to 1776; afterwards it was owned by Greene's brother, Jacob, and his wife, Margaret. It's also home to some paranormal phenomena.

Nathanael Greene has been credited with being the "Savior of the American Revolution" by none other than George Washington himself. It was rumored that when King George asked who the main culprits were in the Revolutionary War military opposing the British Army, his ministers showed him only two portraits: that of George Washington and Nathanael Greene.

Before the war, Greene managed a branch of his father's Iron foundry and also served several terms in the blossoming colonial legislature.

In 1775, a year before independence was officially declared, he was appointed commander of the Rhode Island Army, and in 1776, the official start of the war of independence, he was promoted to Major General. From the beginning of the war Nathanael Greene and George Washington worked very closely together. Greene served with Washington at the Siege of Boston during the years 1775 to 1776, also when fighting broke out around New York.

Among some of the other engagements General Greene participated in were: Trenton, Brandywine, and Germantown. Greene even served as Quartermaster General for Washington at his encampment at Valley Forge and according to most historical accounts, did the best job he could under the extremely barbaric circumstances.

In 1778, Greene replaced General Horatio Gates as Commander of the Southern Armies. It was at this time that Greene's true aptitude as a commander would be sorely tested. His opposition was none other than the famous Lord Cornwallis, who had forces in place that greatly outnumbered Greene's Continental Army.

Greene knew that traditional tactics would be useless against Cornwallis' superior forces, so he developed a strategy that relied on quicker mobility of troops and the ability to outmaneuver the opposing army.

Using local militia, Greene used these "Irregular troops" to keep the Redcoats in an extended front line. Meanwhile, using his main force, he kept luring Cornwallis away from the protection of the coast in an effort to get the British Commander to split up his army. This hit and run tactic worked extremely well for the Patriots. It was what allowed General Daniel Morgan to gain a victory at Cowpens, South Carolina. That's not to say that things were all wine and roses for

Greene at this time in the campaign. He may have helped General Morgan, but he himself lost at the Battle of Guilford Courthouse.

The upside was that even though Cornwallis had won a victory for the British, their forces were too weakened to continue to press on the attack to conquer North Carolina and they actually had to retreat back to Virginia.

Seeing his chance, Greene assumed the offensive, and by June of 1781 had pushed the British back to the South Carolina coast. Greene's actions in the Carolinas made possible the surrender of the British Army under the command of Lord Cornwallis at the Battle of Yorktown, Virginia.

Nathanael Greene's post-war life was one that was beset by a small scandal during his last years, that could quite possibly have led to his early death. As Quartermaster General in the south, Greene was accused of profiteering when the inflation rate required paying extra than was authorized by the army for goods.

What in fact happened was that he supplied the southern army with goods that were made by co-signing notes with an independent contractor who went bankrupt and then died leaving him holding the proverbial bag for the goods.

He denied any wrongdoing and facts otherwise have never been proven to this day. Ironically, Greene did his best to pay off his debts until his death in 1786, which some people have speculated might have been a heart attack induced by the strain of paying off those debts.

Fortunately for him, Nathanael Greene is not best remembered for his financial aptitude, but for his superb military strategy skills for which we can all be thankful for to this day.

Getting back to the focus of this book which is telling ghost tales related to the Revolutionary War, The Nathanael Greene homestead in Cumberland, Rhode Island, where General Greene made his home early in the war, has had several unexplained paranormal incidents happen within its walls. Today it's a National Registry of Historic Places site and a museum open to the public.

People who have visited Spell Hall over the years have had feelings of cold spots where there shouldn't be any. Other people have heard the slamming of doors and disembodied footsteps echoing throughout the building. Witnesses have reported hearing the sound of cannon fire and unearthly screams.

No one knows if it's the spirit of Nathanael Greene or not, but from what people have seen and heard, whoever or whatever is haunting the Nathanael Greene homestead is most certainly not resting in peace.

Connecticut Colony

Connecticut is very much a picturesque image of New England in miniature. Its steepled churches, village greens, and old-fashioned clapboard houses are a subtle reminder of the charm that is present all over New England. But, there's always a dark side lurking around the corner and Connecticut has seen its far share of turmoil and tragedy in its long history, enough to spark a few ghostly tales from the Revolutionary War.

Several significant events happened in the colony of Connecticut during the Revolutionary War. During the first few years of the war, Connecticut was practically full of Tories. A Tory or Loyalist, was an American who remained loyal to the crown of England during the rebellion. A Tory was considered a traitor to America in all respects, and anyone suspected of being a Tory or had been proven to help the redcoats in any way, was generally thrown in prison. In Connecticut, mainly in Hartford, the jails were so full of Tories from their own area that the jails were literally overflowing with them. Not only were the jails filled with Tories from Connecticut, but other colonies sent their Tories there as punishment as well.

Another importance in the war was the landing of a British navel force in Westport, Connecticut, that then marched on to Danbury and torched the city because it had given supplies and aid to the Patriots.

The Haunting of Hale Homestead

"I only regret that I have one life to lose for my country."

~*Nathan Hale*

South Coventry, Connecticut, is the birthplace of one of the first martyrs of the Revolutionary War, Nathan Hale. Strangely enough, the ten-room Nathan Hale Homestead is misnamed. Nathan Hale never actually set foot or lived in the house that bears his name. The house was built in 1776, the same year Nathan was executed by the British, by Deacon Hale, Nathan's father, and Nathan Hale's brothers. True, Nathan was born on the site in a different house. Some of Nathan Hale's belongings are displayed in the house and unbeknownst to the many tourists who visit the homestead, it is reputed to be haunted by the spirits of the Hale Family who have remained attached to the house. The first documented paranormal encounter dates back to 1914.

A man by the name of George Dudley Seymore purchased the old, dilapidated, and vacant Hale Homestead. Seymore was a historian and had an admiration for Nathan Hale, who he considered one of his childhood heroes. Seymore noted in his diary that when he and a friend of his, who remains nameless, arrived at the house on a rainy day, the friend saw the apparition of Deacon Hale looking at them through the window. According to Seymore, his friend was so shaken up by the paranormal encounter that he didn't mention it for several hours and then confessed to being disturbed by the appearance of the spirit.

Over the years, George Dudley Seymore also collected more ghost stories and legends about the Hale Homestead from local residents of South Coventry. Seymore learned that not only did the patriarch of the Hale Family, Deacon Hale, haunt the homestead, but that a female spirit named Lydia also haunted the house.

Lydia Carpenter was one of the Hale family's servants. It's said that she had an ear for gossip and was always trying to collect rumors among the other servants of the homestead. It is quite possible that she stuck her nose where it didn't belong and gossiped about the wrong person and that her curiosity caused her demise. As we don't know when she died or what she died of, this is all mere speculation or "gossip."

Lydia's spirit has been spotted sweeping the upstairs hallway in the wee hours of the morning. Another spirit, which might just be another manifestation of Lydia, is known as the "Woman in White." She's been seen in the kitchen area dressed in white colonial garb, and looks as though she's either straightening up the kitchen or getting ready to start cooking for the day. In Lydia's case, it seems like a woman's work is never done...at least in the afterlife.

Another Hale, this time one of Nathan's brothers, Lieutenant Joseph Hale, is supposed to haunt the great cellar area. Evidently, he likes to clank around in the chains he was forced to wear as a prisoner of war by the British.

According to Seymore, Lieutenant Hale was captured by the British and chained up on a prison ship. Eventually, he was released and returned home to the Hale Homestead where he died of Tuberculosis. It's unclear why he would choose to manifest wearing his prison chains though. Perhaps he's trying to prove a point of some sort. Sometimes it's hard enough to figure out why a living person does something strange; it must be twice as hard for a spirit to get its point across.

In later years, the homestead was occupied by caretakers with the last name of Griffith. Mary Griffith, wife of the caretaker, said that she'd met and knew Mr. Seymore. She believed that he always thought the Hale Homestead was haunted, but then she also added that Seymore had gone to England and had always liked haunted castles and ghosts and such things...

According to the current staff at the Hale Homestead Museum, no one else has seen any spirits, nor have they found any evidence of an active haunting. But, that's usually the official response to any paranormal question.

The Ghostly Lovers and Other Spirits of the Daniel Benton Homestead

The Daniel Benton Homestead is located in Tolland, Connecticut. It was built in 1720 and the brick and wood frame house has hosted the descendants of the Daniel Benton family for many years. Daniel Benton died in 1776, but he had three grandsons who fought in the Revolutionary War. Two of the three grandsons died in battle during the war.

It's the third grandson, Elisha Benton, who is the major player in the paranormal drama that surrounds the Daniel Benton Homestead. While doing his patriotic duty for the young rebel nation, Elisha Benton contracted the dreaded smallpox virus when he became a prisoner of war. Unlike our modern times, there was no smallpox vaccine and it was a very deadly virus that claimed many lives. Before he left for the glory of fighting for his country, Elisha Benton became engaged to a young lass named Jemima Barrows.

Elisha promised to marry her after the war. A prospect that many a young girl was told by her intended across the country. Jemima was bitter-sweetly surprised when only a year after he'd left, Elisha had returned home. The reunion was not the happiest occasion that it should have been because it was marred by the fact that Elisha had returned because of his illness and he was unfit for active duty in the army.

Jemima immediately set about to care for the smallpox-ridden Elisha, but despite all her medical efforts, and the efforts of the family's physician, the virus took its deadly toll and Elisha Benton died in 1777, at the home he was born in. Sadly, the tragedy doesn't end here.

Since Jemima was the primary caregiver of Elisha, and back then they weren't aware of quarantine procedures, she also contracted smallpox. Unlike Elisha, who had Jemima to care for him during his last days, Jemima was not so fortunate. She had no one to care for her and shortly before her eighteenth birthday, she also died.

Because the two lovers were never officially married, social conventions of the period would not allow them to be buried together as a husband and wife. There's a small family cemetery plot on the grounds and both Elisha and Jemima are buried within its confines. To satisfy the morals of the time, but to also show respect for their love, the Benton family had them buried near each other, but separated by a carriage track. So for all eternity, they are so close together yet so far apart. Legend has it that because their bodies are buried apart they are unable to reunite in the afterlife, and both their unhappy spirits walk the halls and wander the rooms of the Daniel Benton Homestead in search of each other and of final rest in each other's arms.

Over the next 200 years, various visitors to the homestead have had a variety of paranormal encounters, both visual and audio in nature. In later years, the homestead had passed out of the hands of the Daniel Benton family and was acquired by the Tolland Historical Society. They opened it as a public historic site in 1969.

Since opening as a museum, many visitors have seen what looks to be a gray shadow or ectoplasm (kind of a shadowy, cloudy form), drifting across the front bedroom. That room just happens to be the very same room where both Elisha Benton and Jemima Barrows died.

Other visitors have detected the sound of someone crying or weeping throughout the house, even though no such person was nearby – at least one that they could physically see. People who have stayed overnight in the house have heard disembodied rapping noises and have seen visions of a colonial soldier walking around the house. Could this possibly be the spirit of Elisha Benton? Maybe. Maybe not. You see, Jemima and Elisha aren't the only afterlife residents of the old homestead.

It seems that after the Battle of Saratoga, some Hessian Soldiers who had surrendered were held under house arrest at the Daniel Benton Homestead to await parole. Evidently, the Hessians liked the area so much that they decided to settle down there after the war. Some of them settled into Tolland and others moved on to Boston. Some people believe that at least one of those Hessians decided he liked the Daniel Benton Homestead so much in his lifetime that he chose to return there and settle in his afterlife.

Not only have visitors inside the house seen strange things, but those outside have as well. Re-enactors of the Revolutionary War have had encampments outside the building and have often reported seeing strange flickering lights coming from inside the building – lights that go on and off when they know no one is inside. Regardless of who's haunting the Daniel Benton Homestead, some visitors would agree that they've had the feeling they're not totally alone.

Paranormal Profile: "Mad Anthony" Wayne Gets Around in the Afterlife

NAME: *General "Mad Anthony" Wayne*
BORN: *January 1, 1745*
DIED: *December 15, 1796*

Beyond a shadow of a doubt, General "Mad Anthony" Wayne has got to be one of the most active spirits from the Revolutionary War...and it's no wonder. He's the only colonial war hero to have two graves. Well, actually let me clarify that. He's the only Revolutionary War hero to be buried in two separate graves, 400 miles apart. If you think that's strange, you don't know half of the wild stories about "Mad Anthony."

As strange as his afterlife may seem, during his lifetime Anthony Wayne really did earn himself the nickname: "Mad Anthony" for a good reason. Anthony Wayne was born on New Year's Day in 1745. His grandfather was originally from Ireland and in 1720 emigrated to Paoli, Pennsylvania, and settled there, building a homestead called Waynesboro. It was here, outside of Philadelphia, in Chester County, that Anthony Wayne was born.

Even as a small child his inclination towards a military life was very evident. As a boy, one of his favorite pastimes was to "play war" with

General "Mad Anthony" Wayne, his spirit really gets around in the afterlife.
Courtesy of Christopher E. Wolf

his friends. Anthony Wayne wasn't much of an academic student, but according to one of his schoolmasters, he had the definite makings of a fine soldier. But, strangely enough, he never joined the military once out of school; he became a land surveyor for Pennsylvania and Nova Scotia.

At the age of twenty-one, he married his fiancée, Polly, and settled down into married life at Waynesboro...or so he thought. During this time, he held several minor local political offices and was actively involved in many of the growing patriotic committees and social clubs. It was the outbreak of the Revolutionary War that finally sparked Anthony Wayne's true calling in life.

With the onset of the war, Wayne soon realized his life's ambition to "play war" for real and plunged headfirst into the struggle for American independence. In January of 1776, Anthony Wayne recruited and organized the 4th Pennsylvania Battalion of Continental Troops and for his effort he was commissioned as its Colonel. He was now Colonel Anthony Wayne, the first of many ranks he would acquire over his long military career.

Waynesboro, the birthplace of "Mad Anthony" Wayne. *Courtesy of Christopher E. Wolf*

Many people think that because of Colonel Wayne's exploits during the Revolutionary War, he earned the name "Mad Anthony." This is true, but there are historians out there who have several versions as to how he got the nickname. One version says he received the nickname because he was always amazing his superior officers and the men under his command by using non-conventional military strategy, and he was said to possess a "mad" cunning, zealous personality.

In fact, Anthony Wayne was so cunning, that at the time of his death, he was the ranking officer in the United States Army.

Another version of how he got his nickname is that Anthony Wayne had a reputation for being reckless, fearless, and daring in battle and his men thought he was "mad" for some of the combat orders he would issue.

But according to some historians there is a totally different reason that he earned the nickname, "Mad Anthony," a reason that had nothing to do with his skill as a commanding officer. One of Anthony Wayne's most daring exploits during the Revolutionary War was his midnight attack on the British troops at Stoney Point, New York. Armed with only their bayonets and the cover of darkness, his forces surprised the British and recaptured the area for the Americans.

It was here that Anthony Wayne gained the nickname – not because of his cunning victory, but because of a near fatal injury.

He was shot in the head by a musket ball. A nearby military surgeon by the name of Absalom Baird rushed to his side, and performed a radical cranial operation called, "cranioplasty."

It's a surgical technique that was first developed back in the seventeenth century where broken skull fragments are removed and replaced with a metal plate. An unfortunate side effect to this operation is that it causes epileptic-like seizures. It was these seizures that would make General Wayne fall to the ground and twist, turn, spasm uncontrollably, and foam at the mouth. That is how he gained the nickname: "Mad Anthony."

General "Mad Anthony" Wayne had so many exploits during his war years that they have literally filled volumes and volumes of books. His military career during the Revolutionary War had many highs, such as the Battle of Stoney Point, and some lows, including The Paoli Massacre, in which he requested and received a court marshal, due to his negligence in camping his men so close to the British lines allowing the Redcoats a chance to repay him for his midnight attack at Stoney Point.

After the war ended, George Washington, in 1792, offered General Wayne command of the regular army with the rank of Major General. His mission was to fight the hostile Native Americans in Ohio. For the next four years, until his death by illness brought on by acute gout, General "Mad Anthony" Wayne was the highest ranking officer in the United States Army. Near death, General Wayne was taken to the blockhouse at Presque Isle in Erie, Pennsylvania, and on December 15, 1796, one of the greatest and most controversial heros of the Revolutionary War was dead...but his "Mad" spirit lives on.

General "Mad Anthony" Wayne's spirit is always on the move and that might be because of the bizarre occurrences surrounding his grave sites and burials. Yes, burials, as in more than one.

On his deathbed, General Wayne in true-to-form fashion, gave his men unusual, but specific instructions as to how he wanted to be buried. He requested to be buried in full, military dress uniform, wearing highly polished boots, and no fancy coffin – just a plain pine box. He also requested to be buried, not in his hometown of Paoli, but at the base of the flagstaff, on Presque Isle, where the blockhouse that he died in was located.

For thirteen years the body of General "Mad Anthony" Wayne lay peacefully in his grave. The same could not be said, however, for his spirit. General Wayne's ghost really does get around in the afterlife. His spirit is said to act out several different roles from his life. Some of his major hauntings include, Lake Memphremagog, Fort

Ticonderoga, an uncompleted house in Virginia, and Storm King Pass in northern New York state. With so many haunted sites, we'll take a look at each one individually starting with Lake Memphremagog.

A VISIT TO THE LAKE

In 1776, General Wayne and two guides from Canada, went to Lake Memphremagog, (try saying that three times fast), to search for a bald eagle nest. General Wayne had heard that if you can catch an eagle young enough, they can be trained and that bald eagles make excellent hunting birds.

Luck was with him, and they found what they were seeking: A bald eagle's nest with not one, but two bald eaglets. Just as General Wayne reached into the nest to gather them up, one of the eaglets lashed out with a claw and scratched him on his cheek and the bridge of his nose, scarring him for life.

General Wayne didn't hold the attack against them. He trained and kept both the eagles for their entire lives and never traveled without them by his side for many years.

After his death, the spirit of "Mad Anthony" was sighted by many trappers and fishermen at the lake over the years. Evidently, Wayne's ghost, dressed as an Indian Scout, has been seen with his arms outstretched with a bald eagle perched on each fist as he glides across the lake with his feet barely touching the water.

THE GENERAL
AT FORT TICONDEROGA

Another place that General "Mad Anthony" Wayne's ghost is said to haunt is Fort Ticonderoga in New York State. He was the fort Commandant in 1771. Not only does he haunt the fort, but when he was in command, he had an affair with a woman named Nancy Coates and she has been seen as well.

It seems she committed suicide by jumping into Lake Champlain when General Wayne turned his romantic intentions towards a young British lass named Penelope Haynes.

The ghost of Nancy Coates has been seen manifesting in and around Fort Ticonderoga and Lake Champlain. When she appears at the lake, her spirit takes the form of a dead body floating face up in the water. Inside the fort, people have heard the disembodied sound of a woman crying her heart out.

General Wayne's spirit has been seen in the fort's dining room and in his old Commandant's quarters. He likes to sit in an old wingback chair, smoking his favorite clay pipe and mimicking the pose in his portrait that hangs in the same room. At other times, "Mad Anthony" has been spotted pacing back and forth along the outside ramparts of the fort that face Mount Defiance.

WAYNE IN THE RUINS

Near Rogues Road in Loudoun County, Virginia, sits the ruins of a half-built, Georgian-style brick house, once owned by Phillip Noland. Noland was a very good friend of General Wayne's and ol' "Mad Anthony" liked to visit Noland on a regular basis to see how the construction was going on the house, which he was very fond of.

Noland was forced to abandon his dream house sometime during the Revolutionary War because he had run out of money to build it any further. All that remains of the house are some ruined unfinished walls and the cellar.

During the war, two Hessian soldiers escaped from the prison camp at Saratoga and sought to hide in the unfinished house. They were tracked down by the Continental soldiers and then executed in the cellar. Their unhappy spirits are said to lurk around the empty half-built structure and to make pounding noises and scratching sounds on the cellar walls in frustration at being trapped there.

The ghost of General Wayne is also known to appear on the premises of the ruins. Since Phillip Noland was a close friend of his, its been speculated that General Wayne's spirit appears here to ponder why the house was never finished.

THE MIDNIGHT RIDE OF... "MAD ANTHONY"?

The ghost of "Mad Anthony" Wayne and his favorite steed, Nab, have been seen riding along the banks of the Hudson River and on the roads between Storm King Pass and Stoney Point, New York. It's the paranormal replay of one of General Wayne's greatest triumphs and the greatest personal tragedy of his military career.

In 1779, General George Washington ordered General Wayne to get word to his troops of an impending British attack at Storm King Pass. Without regard for his own life and limb, General Wayne rode his faithful horse, Nab, through the night during a tremendous, violent thunderstorm and managed to warn the

American troops to prepare for the British attack. Not only did he warn the troops of the impending attack, but he also managed to return to his own troops and lead them in a highly successful, yet risky midnight bayonet charge on the British troops at Stoney Point, New York.

It was at Stoney Point where he was to earn the nickname that stuck with him for the rest of his life.

Local residents say that you can see the ghost of General Wayne riding his horse, Nab, whose horseshoes are said to shoot sparks of orange and blue as they hit the road. The ghost of the General and his beloved horse are said to appear at night just prior to an impending thunderstorm, much like the one General Wayne rode though to alert the American troops.

SERGEANT TROTTER'S CURSE

When President George Washington commissioned "Mad Anthony" Wayne as Commander-In-Chief of the United States Army in 1792, Wayne built a supply port at his Headquarters called Fort Fayette, near the old Fort Pitt in Pittsburgh.

Although there was no lack of opportunity for fighting the Indian Wars, there were periods of peace. General Wayne was a man of action and when he couldn't find any, you could rest assured that he would create some on his own for himself and his troops. One of his major character flaws was that he tended to drink heavily when not engaged in battle. By all accounts, he tended to be a rather nasty-tempered drunk.

A man by the name of Sergeant John Trotter thought he would take advantage of one of General Wayne's drinking binges and figuring he would not be missed at the fort, decided to take an unauthorized leave of absence and visit his home in Murrysville.

Wayne wasn't nearly as drunk as Trotter thought and while he was gone, the General called for him to report for duty. When "Mad Anthony" discovered that he was absent from the fort, he not only became "Mad," but also enraged! In addition, he was feeling thoroughly miserable from a massive hangover. General Wayne ordered three of his officers to locate the missing Trotter and shoot him on site for desertion.

Meanwhile, Trotter was returning from his trip home, unaware that he had a death sentence on his head. As he approached the fort's main gate, Wayne's officers captured him and prepared to carry out their orders.

Not surprising, the officers probably felt some measure of pity and understanding for Trotter and maybe that's why instead of shooting him outright, they allowed him one last request. Trotter asked for a Bible. Flipping through the Bible, he knew exactly what he would do. First, he called down the Lord's vengeance on everyone involved, the three officers and especially General Wayne. Secondly, he recited Psalm 109, *The Prayer of the Falsely Accused*. As he finished saying his prayer, he tacked a curse onto the end of it: "My accusers will be clothed with disgrace and wrapped in shame as in a cloak!" Perhaps Trotter thought that the officers might be frightened enough to let him escape. No such luck.

The officers carried out their orders and executed Trotter on the spot. In hindsight, perhaps the officers should've let Trotter escape, for it seemed that Trotter's curse came to pass after all. One of the officers went insane. He claimed that he was possessed by the devil. Nobody knows of his eventual fate but, back then insane people weren't exactly treated with care or sympathy.

The second officer of the trio became an alcoholic, and while there's nothing supernatural about that – right? – perhaps, he just couldn't handle the guilt on his conscience for Trotter's death. But wait, there's more. For the rest of his life, the unfortunate drunken wretch believed that he was being hounded by Satan in the form of a rabid, mad dog that only he could see...and the third officer?

He was stricken with a particular nasty effect of Trotter's curse, perhaps even the worst of the three. He developed a type of diabetes that made him continually thirsty for the rest of his life.

General Wayne eventually sobered up and became deeply depressed over the Trotter incident. It was also rumored that Trotter's ghost haunted General Wayne and the other officers involved in his death.

THE TWO GRAVES
OF "MAD ANTHONY" WAYNE

General Anthony Wayne died on December 15, 1796, and as per his deathbed request, he was buried at the base of the flagstaff of the blockhouse where he died, on Presque Isle. For thirteen long years his body rested in peace, but it was not to last.

At the request of several family members, Isaac Wayne, the son of Anthony Wayne, traveled along what is now Route 322, all the way to Presque Isle to retrieve his father's remains and have them reburied where they belonged, in the family church graveyard in Radnor, Pennsylvania. Even though it went against his father's last wishes, the family wanted him back home.

Isaac's journey was a grueling 400-plus mile one-way trek and he made the trip in a small, horse-drawn cart, rather than a full-sized wagon in order to make the unpleasant trip go faster. When Isaac Wayne arrived at Presque Isle, he wasted no time in having his father's remains dug up. Unfortunately, he was in for a shock. When they opened the plain, pine coffin, the sight was gruesome, but incredible. The body of "Mad Anthony" Wayne was virtually undecayed after thirteen years of being buried! The only part of him that had decayed was part of one leg.

Author S. B. Nelson, in his book, written a hundred years after the death of General Wayne had this to say about the incident:

> *On opening the grave, all present were amazed to find the body petrified, with the exception of one foot and leg, which were partially gone. The boot on the unsound leg had decayed and most of the clothing was missing. Dr. Wallace separated the body into convenient parts and placed them in a kettle of boiling water until the flesh could be removed from the bones.*

Say What!? They did What? That's right! They took out General Wayne's body from his grave, cut it into manageable pieces, and then cooked the parts in a kettle of boiling water. The reason they did this gruesome act wasn't out maliciousness, but out of practicality. Isaac Wayne's cart was too small to transfer the whole body of his father and rather than getting a larger wagon, he opted to bring home what he could fit in the cart, namely just the bones.

After they packed up General Wayne's bones for transport, they took what was left over, basically his uniform and his flesh in the form of General Wayne soup, and poured it back into his original coffin and reburied it in his original grave.

Isaac Wayne traveled back east towards his home to bury his father's bones in St. David's Churchyard with the rest of the Wayne family.

The ghostly and ghastly part of the story is this: Ever since he was disinterred, the ghost of General Wayne, minus his head, (What is it with Revolutionary War spirits and missing heads?) lurks around the streets of Erie, Pennsylvania, in search of his head.

There's also been sightings of Wayne's ghost seated on a ghostly version of his favorite horse, Nab, riding around the site of his grave at the blockhouse on Presque Isle every night at the stroke of midnight.

One final tale states that when Isaac Wayne made the long trek back to Radnor with his father's bones, they weren't packed as securely as they should have been with the result being that some of them fell out of the box on the bumpy road and were never found. Legend has it that every year, on the anniversary of his birthday, January 1, "Mad Anthony" Wayne's spirit rises from his grave (The one in Radnor, not Presque Isle), and rides his horse, Nab, along Route 322 in search of his missing bones. So, if by chance, you happen to be traveling on Route 322, on New Year's Day and catch a glimpse of a colonial soldier on horseback, don't be alarmed. It's just "Mad Anthony" on his quest to reunite the pieces of his body.

Section Two:

GHOSTLY

MANIFESTATIONS

OF THE MIDDLE

COLONIES

The provinces of New York and Vermont, New Jersey, Pennsylvania, and the Delaware Colony comprise the middle area of the original thirteen colonies. In this section we'll take a paranormal look at some of the famous – and not so famous – battlefields, plantations, and towns that are a awash in colonial history, not to mention ghosts and hauntings of every kind imaginable.

We'll visit sites such as the Old Dutch Church in Sleepy Hollow, New York, where the headless horseman makes his resting place.

In the Province of Pennsylvania we'll take a close look at the battlefield of Brandywine and maybe catch a glimpse of General "Mad Anthony" Wayne. Not to be ignored is the Encampment at Valley Forge where the spirit of George Washington might still visit his old Headquarters for some much needed rest and inspiration. In the Province of New Jersey we'll examine the famous Spy House Museum and Ringwood Manor. We'll visit the Delaware Colony where there's rumors that a werefox operated as a scout for General Lafayette near the Brandywine Creek, and further south we'll examine the ghostly abode of the man who was credited with "penning the Revolution."

The Province of
New York and Vermont

A t least one third of all the major battles of the Revolutionary War were fought within the boundaries of the Province of New York and Vermont. Like many of the other British colonies, New York declared its independence on July 9th, 1776. As with the other colonies that declared their independence, battle with the British army was soon to follow.

As we learned earlier in the book, the Patriots captured cannons and gunpowder from the British at places like Fort Ticonderoga to

The old mill at the outskirts of Sleepy Hollow. *Courtesy of Christopher E. Wolf*

use against them long before the "official" start of the Revolutionary War. New York Province saw military action in the form of several major battles.

One of the first major battles of the war was the Battle of Long Island in 1776. Another pivotal battle fought on New York soil was the Battle of Saratoga. In fact, this battle gave the Continental Army the recognition they were hoping for from France.

There's an abundance of Ghost and hauntings in New York, from the Literary specter of the Headless Horseman to the restless Spirits of Raynham Hall and everywhere in between.

The "Real" Headless Horseman and Other Spirits of the Old Dutch Burying Ground

"Indeed, certain of the most authentic histories of those parts, who have been careful in collecting and collating the floating facts concerning this specter, allege that the body of the trooper, having been buried in the church yard, the ghost rides forth to the scene of battle in nightly quest of his head; and that the rushing speed with which he sometimes passes along the Hollow, like a midnight blast, is owing to his being belated, and in a hurry to get back to the church yard before daybreak."

~Washington Irving
From "The Legend Of Sleepy Hollow"

Let's face it. Unless you've lived in an isolated commune or have been in a coma for most of your life, you've probably heard of the "Legend of Sleepy Hollow" and the Headless Horseman. Almost everyone has probably seen the Disney version of the tale or the more recent live action version starring Johnny Depp from a few years ago.

Regardless of which version you're familiar with, the name Sleepy Hollow just has an ominous ring to it. But, what most people may not realize is that there really is a place named Sleepy Hollow in upstate New York that Washington Irving lived in and used for the basis of his story.

But for anyone who's not familiar with the tale or has forgotten most of it, here's a brief summary: "The Legend of Sleepy Hollow" takes place about thirty years after the Revolutionary War in the town of Sleepy Hollow, New York.

A strange, scarecrow of a man named Ichabod Crane arrives as the new schoolteacher and after settling in to his new surroundings, finds he is attracted to a woman named Katrina Van Tassel. He decides to court her, but there's another townsman who is also courting the lovely Miss Van Tassel, the town blacksmith, Brom Bones.

A very different type of man from the frail, intellectual schoolteacher, Brom Bones is an obnoxious, large, muscular man who is used to getting what he wants, and what he wants is the hand of Katrina Van Tassel.

One night at a party hosted by the Van Tassels and attended by Ichabod Crane and Brom Bones, Bones tells the story of the Headless Horseman who roams the woods and byways of their little community searching for his head and willing to take the head of any unfortunate nighttime traveler who is unfortunate enough to cross his path.

Later that night, while riding his nag home to the schoolhouse, Ichabod Crane crosses paths with the Headless Horseman who pursues him relentlessly throughout the Hollow until they reach a bridge. Unable to cross the bridge, the Horseman throws his head at the fleeing schoolteacher as he crosses the bridge.

The next morning Ichabod Crane is nowhere to be found. The only thing left is a smashed pumpkin near the bridge and Crane's horse. Crane is never seen again in Sleepy Hollow. Was he a victim of the Headless Horseman? Or did he just leave the area in fright, never to return.

Some people in the town speculated that it was never really a ghost chasing Ichabod Crane, that it was his rival, Brom Bones, dressed as the horseman to scare the schoolteacher into leaving town. Another townsfolk member recalls seeing Ichabod Crane in New York City years later. This is the story told by Washington Irving.

Was there really a Headless Horseman in Sleepy Hollow? Let's examine the facts. Washington Irving used real places and people as characters in his stories. He may have exaggerated a few of their personality traits to suit his story, but most of them have a basis in reality. Let's take a look at one of the main characters, if not *the* main character: the Headless Horseman. Who was he? What was he? Where did he come from? All these questions and more we'll attempt to answer. First of all, who was the Headless Horseman?

According to Washington Irving, the Headless Horseman was a Hessian mercenary of an unknown rank, who lost his head having it shot off by a cannonball. The battle took place at Chatterton Hill. Besides the unfortunate horseman, 548 other Hessian soldiers also lost their lives in combat. They buried the headless horseman in an unmarked grave inside the Old Dutch Burying Ground in Sleepy Hollow. No one was ever able to locate his head after the battle, so they buried him without it.

Aside from being a pretty gruesome way to die, the loss of ones head seems to be traumatic for the soul of the unfortunate victim. There are many tales of headless specters, from Ann Boleyn walking the parapets of the Tower of London in England to the more modern tale of the unfortunate Joe Baldwin, a train conductor who loses his head in a train collision. They all have one common goal: to find their missing heads.

The Headless Horseman takes this goal one step further than most headless specters. He not only seeks to find his own head, but is willing to harvest the head of anyone he comes across in his nightly search. Talk about trying to get ahead!

I'm guessing the main goal of the Headless Horseman is to be reunited with his own head so he can finally rest in peace. So why take other people's heads? Perhaps in the cosmic scheme of things when he harvests any head, it gives him a temporary respite from his eternal torment and allows him to rest in peace for a period of time.

In this respect, he has more of the characteristics of a zombie, ghoul, or even a vampire! In fact, if we take a closer look at what the Headless Horseman does in his nightly wandering, it shows that he's something more than just your average run of the mill ghost. He has some strange limitations that are more vampire-like than ghostly.

For example: Most ghosts usually just appear out of thin air and use their ghastly-looking appearance to frighten the unexpected observer. Rarely do they conduct any physical harm to the person they've manifested to, unless because of the fear they've caused the person provides some kind of bodily injury as they attempt to get away from the ghost.

Not so with the Headless Horseman. He goes out of his way to chase down Ichabod Crane and tries to do him direct harm by severing his head like a ripe melon.

Another difference between the Headless Horseman and other ghosts is the fact that he's unable to cross running water. I've never heard of any other ghost that couldn't cross water. This is more directly a similar weakness of a vampire. Vampires are reputed to not be able to cross running water. Hence the action that the Headless Horseman cannot cross the bridge to pursue Ichabod Crane and has to throw a pumpkin or another head at him, makes him more like a vampire than a ghost.

One last final weakness that separates the Headless Horseman from other specters, headless or otherwise, is the mention that he has to be back in his grave before sunrise.

This is very much like a vampire needing to be back in his coffin by sunrise. I have never heard of a ghost that was allergic to sunlight; granted you might not see many in the daytime, but there have been many paranormal encounters with spirits in the daytime and they don't seem to be affected by the sun's rays in the least. So where did Washington Irving come up with the Headless Horseman character?

There are two versions of where he may have gotten the idea. The first version is that supposedly as a young boy growing up in Sleepy Hollow, Washington Irving used to play amongst the tombstones in the Sleepy Hollow Cemetery, not to be confused with the Old Dutch Burying Ground which is a much older cemetery that was around during the Revolutionary War. Irving was known to pester an African-American undertaker who worked in the cemetery. It's been speculated that this undertaker was the person who told him about the legend of the Headless Hessian buried in the Old Dutch Burying Ground and then in later years as a writer, he incorporated the legend for his own use and embellished the tale.

Another possible origin is that the Headless Horseman could be from...New Jersey? That's right, New Jersey. Washington Irving lived in New Jersey for a while, as he researched his biography of George Washington. Irving heard rumors and tales about a Hessian mercenary who lost his head from a cannonball in battle at the Great Swamp region of Morris and Somerset counties in New Jersey.

Several years ago, I decided to take a haunted tour of New England for a week. The number one spot on my list of locations to visit was Sleepy Hollow, New York. I had already done some research on the area, but going there would be one of the highlights of my trip. I was not planning on using the time on vacation as any sort of paranormal investigation; it just merely was time to get away and visit the places I had only read about in books.

The day I left home was not the best day of weather. It was mid October and it had been raining on and off for several days. I knew I had at least a five-hour drive and was hopeful that the weather would improve as I drove further north towards New York. As luck would have it, the weather did change from a downpour of rain and wind to just a slight drizzle and some fog. As I reached the area of White Plains, New York, not far from Tarrytown and the suburb of Sleepy Hollow, I could feel the anticipation growing in me of what I

Despite it's serene appearance, the town of Sleepy Hollow has seen the horrors from the Revolutionary War. *Courtesy of Christopher E. Wolf*

would find there. Could the area possibly be as haunted as I've always imagined? Would the locals be willing to talk about any paranormal experiences they've encountered or would the area just be touristy and a complete let-down? These were the questions running through my mind as I turned onto the Tappen Zee Bridge and drove into the heart of the Hudson Valley.

My first impression of Tarrytown and Sleepy Hollow was somewhat disappointing. The driving rain had returned as I drove into town and located the bed and breakfast I'd be staying at for the next several days as I explored the surrounding town and countryside.

After settling in at The Crowe's Nest B&B, which was a tidy little cottage run by a retired husband and wife in their 90s, I set out to get acquainted with Tarrytown and Sleepy Hollow. I felt that I was on the right track after driving around in the rain through the twisty winding streets of Tarrytown. How can you go wrong ghost hunting in a town called Sleepy Hollow? I was amused by the signs for Sleepy Hollow High School and their school's mascot that was none other than our old friend, the Headless Horseman!

In the town's visitor center I bought some local lore books and picked up a map of the Old Dutch Burying Ground. This was the pay dirt information I was looking for: It had everything I wanted to know about the "Legend of Sleepy Hollow" and the Headless

Horseman. There were the usual touristy knick-knacks scattered throughout the store, including Headless Horseman T-shirts and baseball caps but I resisted the urge to buy anything. It just wasn't my thing. I was more interested in getting closer to where all the paranormal action was happening.

Despite, the bad weather (it rained for the next two days straight), I was determined to do some paranormal investigating. After all, I hadn't driven for hours to get here just to sit in my room and read about places that were nearby. I compromised by going to indoor haunted locations.

One of the best places I visited was Lindhurst Mansion. Granted this is a book on Revolutionary War hauntings, but if you ever get the chance, go visit Lindhurst. It's a great example of what kind of home wealth could buy you in the early twentieth century.

The House was actually used as the site of Collinswood Mansion on the supernatural-themed television soap opera, *Dark Shadows* in the 1970s. It's also really haunted as well.

Finally, on my third and last day in Sleepy Hollow, the rain finally stopped and I was able to go and investigate some of the outdoor haunted sites of Sleepy Hollow, not to mention being able to retrace the hurried ride of Ichabod Crane in his haste to get away from the Headless Horseman.

Thanks to my Visitor's Center map, I was able to locate the spot where Ichabod Crane first crosses paths with the Headless Horseman. It wasn't hard to do. You see, not only is the spot a local park, complete with swing sets and sliding boards, but it also has a large monument directly alongside the entrance.

This is Patriot's Park. The monument doesn't have anything to do with the "Legend of Sleepy Hollow" although it does pertain to the Revolutionary War. This plaque and monument marks the spot where the British spy, Major John Andre, was captured carrying the stolen plans for West Point that were given to him by the traitor, Benedict Arnold. Washington Irving mentions this exact spot in his narrative telling about the location where Ichabod Crane meets the Headless Horseman and then the chase back to the Old Dutch Burying Ground.

"It was at this identical spot that the unfortunate André was captured, and under the covert of those chestnuts and vines were the sturdy yeomen concealed who surprised him."

~Washington Irving
"The Legend of Sleepy Hollow"

The next location I visited was called the Headless Horseman's Bridge. This is the bridge that supposedly the Headless Horseman couldn't cross to pursue the fleeing Ichabod Crane. The road that Ichabod Crane raced down to get away from the Headless Horseman used to be called the Albany Post Road, but a for a very long time, it's been rerouted and is now known as Broadway. In fact, again Washington Irving mentions this in "The Legend of Sleepy Hollow":

"The bridge became more than ever an object of superstitious awe, and that may be the reason why the road has been altered of late years so as to approach the church by the border of the mill pond."

Originally, the road passed the Old Dutch Burying Ground on the west side of the church, but later they changed the route so that it now passes on the east side. Not much of a difference to you and I, but to the Headless Horseman, it may make a bit of difference considering he has to get back to his grave in the church yard by sunrise so the story goes; that means he'd have to change his route a bit. The original bridge is gone, but in the Sleepy Hollow Cemetery there's another wooden bridge that spans a small river that they call the Headless Horseman's Bridge. It's not far from the Old Dutch Burying Ground where his grave lies, so I guess one bridge is good as another.

The Olde Dutch Burying Ground, lair of the infamous Headless Horseman.
Courtesy of Christopher E. Wolf

It was shaping up to be a nice cool October day as I finally made my way to the highlight of my route through Sleepy Hollow: The Old Dutch Burying Ground itself.

I was impressed with the way the graveyard looked. It was easy to see why Washington Irving used this hallowed ground as a location in this story. It's got a very high stone wall, gnarled ancient oak trees, and a multitude of meandering cobblestone footpaths scattered amongst old weathered tombstones. In the bright light of the day, it was a quaint, calm retreat not very far from the main road of Route 9. Not very scary at all.

The more frightening looking graveyard was the larger, Sleepy Hollow Cemetery that adjoined the Old Dutch Burying Ground at one end.

As I wandered through the graveyard, looking for the grave of the Headless Horseman, I noticed an old man dressed in overalls walking directly towards me. He had a look of someone who belonged here, perhaps a maintenance worker or grounds keeper. I walked over to him and introduced myself. On close, inspection he reminded me of Rip Van Winkle, another of Washington Irving's literary characters. He explained that he was the deacon of the Old Dutch Church and that normally he only gave walking tours on Saturdays and Sunday afternoons, but since I had traveled such a distance he'd make an exception and give me the ten-cent tour.

There were a few other people wandering around the cemetery, but they didn't seem interested in getting a tour, so I had the guide all to myself for questioning. He asked me what my interest was in the old burying grounds and I told him that I was interested in "The Legend of Sleepy Hollow" connection. He gave me a grin and said he'd had a feeling that's what I was after. He led the way over to a set of tombstones and pointed to the top of them.

"See those faces with wings?" he asked.

I looked at the stones. There was a peculiar carving at the top of them. If you looked at them at a certain angle of sunlight, they almost looked three dimensional and appeared as though they were hovering over the tomb.

My guide continued, "That's supposedly where young Washington Irving got the idea for a ghost story that would eventually become 'The Legend of Sleepy Hollow.' He would sit in the church on Sunday during a sermon and get bored and daydream. As he looked out the window over there." He pointed at one of the church windows. "And he saw how the sunlight made the faces look on the tombstones, and that gave him the idea."

Okay, I thought, this is the third version I've heard of how the story came to be written. "But, what about the actual grave of the Headless Horseman?" I asked.

He grinned again and led me over to the back side of the church near the stone wall that ran alongside Lincoln Avenue and stopped at an area devoid of markers or tombstones. He pointed down, "This may or may not be the grave you're looking for. Legend has it that a Hessian mercenary is buried in this spot."

He thought for a second and then continued, "In November of 1777, a party of British and Hessian soldiers went on a raiding party in this area. They targeted the wealthy Van Tassel farms as one of their looting parties. The Van Tassels' didn't give up without a fight. When the British commanding officer realized they were resisting, he ordered the farms to be put to the torch to burn the rebels out. At least they had the decency to help the family escape before burning the house down. Horrifically, Elizabeth Van Tassel realized that her one daughter, Baby Leah was still missing! She tried to go back into the house but was repelled by the heat and flames. A Hessian mercenary calmed her down and lead her to a shed, where the baby was safe and sound. He also helped her to hide nearby until all the fighting was over. It is this kind-hearted soldier who is reputed to be buried in the Old Dutch Burying ground, but how he was made out to be the Headless Horseman is still a mystery."

Before I could ask him any more questions, a couple approached us with a problem. They were also touring the graveyard and had run into some car trouble. Their car's battery had just died right outside the entrance to Washington Irving's burial site and asked if we could help them by giving the car a jump start. At the time I didn't think anything strange about the situation, but since then, I've had a chance to think on it.

The man who claimed to be the Dutch Church Deacon, who had been giving me information on the Headless Horseman, claimed that his pickup truck was just over the hill in the parking lot and that he had jumper cables and would help the young couple out. I said I'd come along and help, but he said he was fine on his own.

I walked to the couples car with them to wait for the Deacon. After the few minutes that it would have taken the Deacon to return, I decided to look for his truck. I thought he might need help after all. When I got over the small hill to the parking lot, there was no sign of the Deacon or his truck.

There were a few other people sitting in the lot, so I asked them if they had seen either a red truck or a man matching the Deacons description. No one saw a truck or the man, and they had been there at least a half an hour eating lunch. As far as they knew, no red truck had been parked there when they'd arrived.

By this point I was confused. There's no way a red truck could've left the lot without us seeing it on the hillside, while we were waiting – of that I'm sure. If no one saw the old man leave or arrive in the parking lot from the graveyard, then where did he go?

I finally moved my car up the hill and helped the couple jump start their car and get them on their way. But I couldn't leave well enough alone about this " Deacon" I had been talking to earlier. I searched around the church some more and found someone else connected with the Dutch Burying Ground working in the office. I inquired about the old man who had said he was the Church Deacon and got a very surprising answer – an answer I wasn't sure I could believe.

The clerk said that there *was* a church deacon and that he wasn't very old and certainly didn't sound like the one I'd described to him. So I thought, maybe I heard the guy wrong, but I was sure he'd said he was the Church Deacon. So I asked the clerk if there were any other church deacons and he said there was only one that he knew of and it wasn't the person who I'd described.

Taking a leap of logic I asked if there were any pictures of the church deacons and he showed me a photo album of some of the church deacons past and present. I spotted the man I had seen in the churchyard halfway through the book. I don't normally see ghosts as much as I like to write about them but this was one of those rare occasions where art imitates life. I had just spent a few minutes talking to a spirit and I didn't even know it. At least I knew I wasn't crazy or had hallucinated it because the couple whose car broke down had seen him as well.

The reason I say I had seen a ghost is because, even though the man was the Deacon of the Church, he was a *former* Deacon who had died several years ago. So even though I had been searching for a famous ghost, the Headless Horseman. I guess I can say I wasn't disappointed because I actually was able to speak to a less famous spirit, the Old Deacon.

The Restless Spirits of Raynham Hall

The spirit of Major John André could very well be the most well recognized ghost on Long Island and his spirit has resided at Raynham Hall for the past 200 or so years. Furthermore he's not the only Revolutionary War spirit in attendance at the old manor.

Raynham Hall was originally called "The Homestead" when it was purchased in 1738 by a man named Samuel Townsend. At that time it wasn't the sprawling twenty-room mansion that it is today. Back then it was a mere four-room frame house. But Samuel Townsend had big plans for the small house. By 1740, it was twice the size of the original with adding four rooms onto the back of the house to make room for a large family of eight children. Raynham Hall is located in the Town of Oyster Bay on Long Island.

In the early days of the Revolutionary War it was by law that homeowners quarter British troops in their homes whether they wanted to or not...mostly not. The Townsends had to play host to the troops along with British Lieutenant Colonel John Simcoe. When Oyster Bay was under British occupation, a gentleman by the name of Major John André was a regular lodger at Raynham Hall in 1778. It's in this house that the seeds of his downfall and ultimately his death were first planted.

John André was born in 1750 in London. Evidently, as a child he must've received a varied education, because as an adult he was credited with being a favorite in high society. According to his peers, he could draw and paint and cut intricate silhouettes in paper. He was also said to be lively company and could tell stories and could sing and recite poetry.

At the age of twenty he enlisted in the British army and was assigned to the 23rd Foot Regiment in Canada with the rank of Lieutenant. He was captured a year later at Fort Saint-Jean and for some reason was transported to my home town of Lancaster, Pennsylvania, to be held prisoner for the next year. He was probably either held in the old jail under the Fulton Opera House or at some estate – perhaps Edward Hands, under house arrest. Regardless of where he was kept, he was exchanged for another prisoner. The fact that he was captured must not have affected his military career, because not long afterward he was promoted to Captain in the 26th Foot, and then in 1778, he was promoted to Major. In 1779, he became an Adjutant General of the British army with the rank of Major and was made the head of British Secret Intelligence. Major André made a critical mistake in not taking the patriotism of the Townsend family seriously – that or they hid it well.

In any case, Major André was discussing his plans for paying Benedict Arnold in gold for his turning over the plans for West Point to them and becoming a traitor to the patriot cause. Benedict Arnold would surrender his troops with no resistance to Major André in exchange for the gold. Blood money of the first order.

Unbeknownst to the two British plotters, one of Samuel Townsend's daughters overheard the plot and informed her father, who immediately relayed the message to General Washington. Eventually, Major André was captured in Sleepy Hollow at the exact same spot that Washington Irving placed the fatal first encounter between Ichabod Crane and the Headless Horseman in "The Legend of Sleepy Hollow."

The traitor, Benedict Arnold, managed to escape on a British ship, but poor André was not so lucky. Having been captured as a spy, he was treated as one. At least he was given a fair trial by Washington and his generals, unlike the unfortunate Nathan Hale from four years earlier by the British. Ultimately though, Major André was made an example of what would happen to other British spies should they be caught on American soil. He was hanged at the gallows and his body was buried underneath them for several years until his remains were later disinterred and returned back to England for a proper burial.

Major André's spirit, however, is still thought to have remained at Raynham Hall – his home away from England during the war. Evidently, he very much liked the hospitality of Raynham Hall and was known to have frequented it even before the war between England and the United States had even started. Perhaps his spirit hasn't realized that his mortal remains are no longer on American soil or maybe he no longer cares after 200 years.

Major André's ghost has been spotted wandering the halls of the now-restored mansion; since it was turned into a state museum, many visitors and staff have spotted a colonial-looking specter that bears a distinct resemblance to Major André.

There's also a few more spirits that call Raynham Hall home. Another British soldier has been seen in the house and the legend goes that he may have kept a lover secreted there during the years of the Revolutionary War. Whether it was one of Samuel Townsend's daughters or someone else entirely has yet to be discovered. It was said that one of the bedrooms where this spirit has manifested is colder and always has a chill to it.

Additional paranormal activities in Raynham Hall include orbs and other ectoplasm captured on film. Strange smells such as someone baking or cooking when in fact no meals are even being prepared in the vicinity.

The Raynham Hall Museum is open to the public year-round, so you might actually have a good chance of capturing some ghostly activity on your visit.

The Province of New Jersey

Th e Province of New Jersey has a sort of split personality when it comes to the Revolutionary War. As far back as 1765, colonists from New Jersey were not happy with the way they were being taxed by England and weren't afraid to show it. They burned the royal stamp tax collector in effigy to show their displeasure. He ended up being forced to resign in shame (or fear for his life).

By the late 1770s, the colony was fighting a civil war amongst itself as family and friends began splitting into groups of either Rebels or Loyalists.

At the start of the Revolutionary War, the battalions of New Jersey Loyalists fighting for the British equaled the number of New

Courtesy of Cindy Wolf

Jersey volunteers fighting in George Washington's Continental Army. Even one of the signers of the Declaration of Independence from New Jersey, a man named Richard Stockton, signed a British loyalty oath.

Many of the Loyalists in New Jersey fled to British-controlled New York for their own safety at the start of the Revolution. Because of all the battles fought in New Jersey and because it was located in a central location in the colonies, the Province of New Jersey became known as: "The Crossroad of the Revolution."

From Saddle River to Cape May, New Jersey has its fair share of haunted locations and several of them are Revolutionary War related.

The Spirits of the Spy House Museum

The Spy House Museum in Port Monmouth, New Jersey, is probably one of the finest examples of Classical Colonial architecture on the eastern seaboard. It's also one of the most haunted with over seventy different documented cases of paranormal activity.

One of those cases I can personally vouch for. But before I get talk about what my connection to the Spy House Museum is, I'd like to talk about some of the history of the building and some of the other paranormal activity that has occurred over its long history.

The Spy House was built in 1696 by a man named Daniel Seabrook, a planter who took his inheritance of eighty pounds of sterling and bought 202 acres of property from his stepfather, Thomas Whitlock. It was to be a grand legacy and the plantation remained in the hands of the Seabrook Family for the next 250 years, as they alternately worked the land and sailed ships from the nearby harbor.

So what does this have to do with the Revolutionary War? Quite a bit as you'll soon find out. The House earned the nickname: "The Spy House" by the British Army in 1778.

The Revolutionary War was in full gear as the British were busy marching through Middletown, New Jersey and looting, pillaging, and burning houses and villages. Not to sit on their hands and allow this to happen uncontested, the Monmouth Militia banded together in cooperation with the men who operated the whaling boats to see what they could do to disrupt the English shipping lines in the area.

It was George Washington, who canvassed the area for a volunteer to spy on the British in the harbor.

A man by the name of John Stillwell, a corporal in the Continental Army volunteered for the task. He took a position on Garrett's Hill not far away from the Spy House and easily the highest point in the area to spy from without being caught.

Corporal Stillwell didn't have an easy task ahead of him. Aside from the British and American front lines constantly moving back and forth in flux as one battle was lost or won by either side. He also had to contend with the fact that some of his own close relatives were Tories, loyal to the British, and if he said the wrong thing at the wrong time it would jeopardize the Patriots, not to mention forfeit his own life. But despite the hazards, he still managed to do an excellent job of spying on the British.

He was able to send specific information to the patriot militia which in turn they could use to form attacks on the British fleet.

One of Stillwell's allies was Major Seabrook, owner of the house that was to soon be known for the rest of time as the Spy House. As far as we know, Seabrook wasn't a spy although he was loyal to the American cause.

It was Stillwell's son, seventeen-year-old Obadiah, who was the main messenger of information to the Patriots.

During one point of his spying mission, Stillwell observed more than a thousand British ships off the New Jersey coastline – prime targets for the Americans. Even though at this time the Patriots had no navel forces to speak of, a stunning twenty-three navel battles were fought between the British and the local militia's whaleboat crews. Finally, the British knew that there had to be some sort of spying being conducted in the area. How else were these rag-tag rebel boats able to out maneuver the mighty British fleet? They cut orders to find the spy and put an end to their ring.

Search parties were dispatched to the area and after a less than thorough search, they declared the house owned by Major Seabrook, a well-known patriot supporter, the Spy House. They never figured out that the spy was really John Stillwell. Convinced of their guilt, the British ordered the Seabrook Homestead burnt to the ground. The house was eventually rebuilt, but with its rebuilding it also gained the new name: The Spy House.

It's been said that the Spy House is one of the most haunted houses in the nation; it's certainly one of the most famous. Technically, the house is located in Keansburg, New Jersey, very close to Middletown. The address is 119 Port Monmouth Road, but everyone usually refers to it as The Spy House.

Many different spirits have manifested in the house. They range from a colonial woman in white who has been seen gliding down the stairs to a remorseful man's spirit trapped in the house because he spied on his neighbors to the British.

The Spy House has been many things over the years: a family home, A Public House or Inn, where important meetings took place concerning the town, and at one point, it finally became a museum in the late 1960s.

I first visited The Spy House Museum in 1976. It was on one of my first overnight camp outs when I was in scouts. It was also to turn out to be one of my first encounters with the paranormal. At the time I visited The Spy House, it was open to the public and the tours were given by an elderly woman by the name of Gertrude Neidlinger.

Ms. Neidlinger and her brother Travis were the curators of The Spy House Museum. The Spy House was the perfect place for a scout troop to camp. The house looked spooky enough, and not only did it look ghostly, there was an added bonus of their being a small shipwrecked vessel lying on its side in the backyard right in the middle of where we had pitched our pup tents for the weekend. The whole location just asked to be explored.

What kid could resist looking around a scary old house and shipwreck? To me it was a scene straight out of a Hardy Boys novel or an episode of Scooby Doo. To my pre-teenaged mind the place just had to have a mystery waiting to be solved!

We were given a personal tour of the inside of The Spy House the first day we arrived by Gertrude Neidlinger. I don't remember whether it was me or one of my fellow scouts who finally popped the question as we were touring the upstairs hallway of the old colonial mansion. "So, is this place haunted?" someone asked from our group. "Yeah, are there any ghosts here?" someone else chimed in.

Not surprised by the questions in the least, Ms. Neidlinger replied, "Well, some people think there are ghosts here." She continued, "I've seen some things that make me think there are. I've also felt some things, too."

As we walked into the first bedroom on the left she said, "This room used to be the boy's room of the Seabrook family. People have heard a baby crying in the corner of this room when there was no one else around." She smiled, "I've heard the crying too." She then held out her right arm. "Any woman who walks in this room, including myself, has had the hairs on their arms and the back of their necks stand on end."

Taking a close look at her arm we did see that the hairs were standing up. It was enough to give you goosebumps.

"Many times when I've been alone in the house, locking it up for the day, I'd get the distinct feeling that I was not alone," Gertrude said, "I've seen the apparition of a lady dressed in white colonial clothing walk down from the attic and come into this room and tuck in a crib and then disappear. I think it might be the spirit of Mrs. Seabrook." That having been said she went on to tell us of the history of the house and of the many seafaring artifacts that are displayed in the different upstairs rooms. The largest room in the upper area of the house was dedicated to artifacts of the whaling ships that plied the nearby waters.

Secretly, even before we were told that the house would be left open for us to use the restrooms at night, we knew that we would have to do our own paranormal investigation later that night when everyone else was asleep.

I was looking forward to actually going into an authentic haunted house at night. Myself and four others waited until the last of the campfires were put out that night. We kept it secret among ourselves that we were going to explore The Spy House at night, looking for ghosts. Not because we were afraid of being laughed at – that wasn't a concern – we just didn't want a whole crowd of people following us into the house and getting in our way and possibly scaring off any spirits we might encounter.

I would like to say that I was the leader of the expedition, but I wasn't. I was just glad to be tagging along with some of the others. We really were allowed to be in the house to use the restrooms, but we were told not to go upstairs and wander around because they didn't want us to accidentally break one of the artifacts. Small chance of that happening.

After hearing the ghost stories about the upstairs Lady in White, that's exactly where we were going to go. I'm not sure what we hoped to accomplish besides seeing a ghost with our own eyes. None of us had any experience in paranormal investigating or had even heard of anyone doing it. This was years before Gettysburg had any ghost tours or the *Ghost Hunters* show was on television. Even the movie *Ghostbusters* wouldn't be released until eight years later.

So there we were. Five scouts, armed with only flashlights and a curiosity for the unknown. As I look back on it now, we really weren't prepared for what happened, I think none of us really expected to encounter a ghost, but we wanted the bragging rights to say we actually went inside a haunted house in the middle of the night. To be honest, I think we spent more time scaring ourselves than the house ever scared us.

Every little creak and moan of the floorboards seemed amplified in the dark. We were all on edge. We made our way up the small back staircase to the second floor, the only light coming from our flashlights. I'm sure that anyone outside the house would've been easily able to see the beams and would know what we were up to, but none of us felt brave enough to go wandering around in the dark.

Once we reached the second floor, we peeked into the Boy's Room where Ms. Neidlinger said she saw the Lady in White. So far we hadn't heard any baby crying nor did we see anything come down from the attic. Maybe we were too early in the night. That or the spirits didn't want to show themselves to outsiders such as ourselves.

We looked into each room up until the last room at the end of the hall. That was the largest room. It also contained the most artifacts. I was one of the first people in the room. I scanned my flashlight over the wooden cases that held the history of whaling, and suddenly I froze. I stopped my light on one of the cases that had held tools used in whaling. Why? Because I saw something or someone move – and it wasn't one of my friends.

They were still standing in the hall behind me. I couldn't make out what had moved from where I was standing in the doorway so I moved closer to the case. At that point I wasn't scared, just curious at what I'd seen move.

As I walked slowly closer, my friends entered the room and started spreading out. What occurred next happened so fast that it's hard to remember what exactly what took place and I'm sure my friends all have their own version of what happened that summer night in The Spy House.

I saw in the beam of my flashlight something roll all by itself across the wooden case and land on the wooden floor with a loud clunk! The noise grabbed the attention of my fellow scouts and in an instant the warm summer night became icy cold in that room.

What I, and no doubt, we all saw was a spar pin, the kind you see in pirate movies; it was kind of a wooden stick with a handle. We saw the spar pin roll off the case onto the floor and start spinning around in a circle in sort of a spectral version of spin the bottle. The thing is, none of us were out of sight of each other and none of us had touched anything in the room, including that spar pin. The only thing that jumped into my mind at that moment was: A ghost must've moved it! The second thing that I did and without really thinking at this point was to yell and run back out of the room.

My friends followed suit right after me. At that point we didn't even stop to catch our breaths in the hall; we just continued to run down the hall and down the steps.

At the bottom of the steps was the back door of The Spy House. I knew if we made it that far, we'd be safe. My only goal at the time was to: Get through that door! The other scouts were right on my heels as we zoomed down the stairs, not caring how much noise we made in the process. A few more feet and we'd be through the door and into the arms of safety!

I reached for the knob and pushed the door open, easily. Too easily, it seemed. I thought the door would be heavier. Turns out I was right. It was a Dutch Door. One that opened at the top and bottom on a hinge. I had just realized that the bottom half of the door was in place when I slammed into it with my stomach and then fell headfirst over the bottom half of the door.

I grunted as the wind was knocked out of me by the impact. Unfortunately, the scout behind me also failed to notice that the door wasn't open the rest of the way and before I could warn him, he too hit the door and fell over the side right on top of me, knocking even more wind out of my lungs.

The others also hit the door but by that time I had managed to get myself out of the way and lay nearby in the sand trying to catch my breath. Thankfully, all the noise hadn't woken anybody else up and we decided to go back to our tents and call it a night.

The next morning, I looked in the room with the spar pin as soon as I got up. Nobody had been upstairs, but the pin was back where it belonged. Nothing was out of place.

A few years later, I was watching a TV show called *Real People*. It was a prime time show on NBC where they would do segments on outrageous people doing crazy things, but every year around Halloween, they'd do a special on haunted places and one of the places they covered was The Spy House. I recognized the place right away. It turns out that The Spy House is one of the most notoriously haunted houses in America.

Hans Holzer, the famous paranormal investigator wrote about his visit to The Spy House. It turns out he was there the same year I was in 1976. Only he was there in the wintertime and I was there in the summer.

In later years, more ghost stories would originate from The Spy House. Here are just some of the paranormal events that have occurred over the years: A year before I visited the Spy House, some other boys were taking a tour and in the same room where the white lady manifests herself, a sewing machine in the room popped open its lid and then the pedals started working all by themselves. One of the boys claimed to see the apparition of a white-bearded old man in the mirror across the room from the sewing machine. Like my friends and I, they ran out of the house and vowed to never return.

A lady who worked as a volunteer in the museum, refused to do any typing in one of the rooms on the second floor because she claimed a draft always went by and knocked her papers to the floor all the time, even when the windows were closed.

A man, similar to what the boys saw in the room with the sewing machine, has been spotted staring down the steps at people and then vanishing into thin air. People claim to hear footsteps from all over the house at once, and the sound of someone breathing has been heard even though there is never anyone around.

There was a time when you could actually go on a ghost tour of The Spy House Museum, but no longer. Shortly before Gertrude Neidlinger died, the Board of Directors relieved her of her position of Curator and also put an end to the ghost tours.

From what I understand now, you can only view the museum from the outside at night. But who knows, you might get lucky and catch a glimpse of one of the many spirits peering out the window.

Ringwood Manor

About an hour's drive from New York City, near Saddle River, New Jersey, sits historic Ringwood Manor. The reason I've included it in this book on Revolutionary War ghosts is two fold. One, it's a building that was once owned by George Washington's geographer; it has historic significance dating back to the war of independence. The other reason is that several of the paranormal occurrences link back to incidents that happened during the war.

Built on land that was used for iron smelting, it was originally owned by the Ogden Family. Iron smelting was a profitable industry during the Revolutionary War and the Patriots needed the iron to make cannonballs and cannons. Robert Erskine was George Washington's geographer or mapmaker, during the Revolutionary War. Old George himself actually used Ringwood Manor several times as a Headquarters.

After the war, General Robert Erskine bought Ringwood Manor. At the time he purchased the house, it was still a relatively small dwelling. He expanded the house and added several rooms. The House has changed owners several times over the past 200-plus years. Even the one-time Mayor of New York, Abraham S. Hewett, was an owner of the property. It was the Hewetts that added the extensions

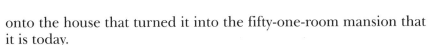

onto the house that turned it into the fifty-one-room mansion that it is today.

In 1936, the state of New Jersey acquired the house and it is now a public museum. Not only did New Jersey inherit the house, they also inherited several spirits attached to the house and grounds. One of the most famous haunts of Ringwood Manor is the Ringwood Cemetery. It's none other than Robert Erskine's spirit that makes his presence known in a rather unique way. Ever since a few months after he died, people noticed that the bricks and mortar on his tomb seemed to be disturbed and chipped away at. Not by vandals as you would have expected. No, the chips and missing bricks seemed to be originating from inside the tomb itself.

According to local historians, sometime during the 1800s, a brick popped out of Erskine's tomb and released his spirit on the unsuspecting world. Ever since that time, many people have spotted his faintly glowing form sitting on top of the his last resting place, holding a lantern, a lantern with the unusual characteristic of glowing with an eerie blue light. Erskine also manifests on his tomb as a glowing blue orb. For some reason he only haunts the cemetery. He's never been spotted inside Ringwood Manor as he seems to prefer the great outdoors. But, you just can't go and expect to see his spirit on just any night you please. General Erskine seems to be limited to showing himself only on the darkest of nights when the moon isn't visible at all.

A few years ago, after hearing a lecture on Ringwood Manor hauntings, three young men decided to test the legend of Erskine's ghost out for themselves. Fortunately for them it wasn't too far from where they lived and they actually did wait until the next dark and moonless night to pursue their investigation. After spending a few hours sitting and joking about the whole ghost nonsense, they decided to leave and rest safe knowing that it was all bunk.

That's when they noticed a faint glow coming from the top of Erskine's tomb. One of the more adventurous of the trio decided that someone was playing a prank on them and decided to take a closer look at the tomb to see if he could find any hidden light source or wires.

As he approached the opposite side of the tomb one of his fellow Ghosthunters screamed: "Look it's moving! Run!" As he turned back he saw the blue light drifting towards his friends who at the same time were making a beeline for their car. He suddenly decided that he didn't want to be left behind and dashed for the car as well, jumping into the back seat as the driver kicked over the ignition.

"Look, there it is!" said the front seat passenger as he pointed at the glowing blue light that hovered in front of the car.

"Yeah," said the driver, quickly shifting into reverse and hitting the gas pedal, "and here we go!"

They quickly vacated the cemetery, and as they were leaving, the ball of light followed them to the edge of the cemetery grounds and then vanished into thin air as they crossed through the gate and into safety, their hearts beating a mile a minute.

Once they got home, they hurriedly called the lecturer and told her what had happened to them at the tomb of Robert Erskine. They were afraid that whatever it was that had followed their car had followed them home as well. She assured them that they were quite safe and that there was no record of the ghost of Robert Erskine ever leaving the confines of the Ringwood Cemetery. Even with the assurance of the lecturer they still vowed never to set foot in the Ringwood Cemetery in daytime or especially at night.

General Robert Erskine's spirit isn't the only haunt of Ringwood Manor over the years; many people have detected supernatural activity in the mansion. This isn't surprising considering that not only did Ringwood Manor have a use as George Washington's temporary headquarters, it also served as a Revolutionary War hospital.

Reportedly, many soldiers died on the grounds of the Manor as their wounds were mortal. Specifically, a significant number of French soldiers are buried in a mass grave that is still sunken from the burial. Disembodied voices speaking in French have been heard near this mass grave site. French soldiers aren't the only auditory manifestations that are heard on the grounds.

People have heard the sound of horses' hooves from the direction of the bridge and have even smelled the pungent odor of horse manure wafting out of the fields across from the manor. The scary part is, no horses have been on the grounds for at least a hundred years.

Even the famed paranormal investigator Hans Holzer has visited Ringwood Manor. He brought a psychic named Ethel Johnson Myers and she claimed to have made contact with the unfriendly spirit of Mrs. Erskine who told them in no uncertain terms to vacate her property.

Another victim of Mrs. Erskine's temper is the unhappy spirit of Jeremiah. He was a family servant who claimed to have been mistreated by Mrs. Erskine while he was alive and living in the manor. Why he's chosen to remain behind in a place that was not a happy one is yet to be discovered. Some spirits return to where they are emotionally tied to complete some unfinished business. Perhaps that's the case with Jeremiah.

The people who work on staff at Ringwood Manor have been some of the best witnesses to the paranormal activity that occurs there. One of the chief witnesses is the superintendent of the manor, Alexander Waldron.

Waldron has claimed to have heard footsteps echoing through the manor when he was positive no one else was around. In fact, he has heard two different sets of footsteps which would probably indicate, as we already know, that there are more than one spirit haunting the manor.

Other staff members have found that doors that were locked up securely the night before would be found wide open the next morning when no one who was employed there could have opened them. They've also noticed the feeling as if a presence was watching them in various parts of the manor house.

So if you're adventurous enough and lucky enough to catch the spirits on an active day, which seems to be quite often around Ringwood Manor, you might just come face to face with one of their many spirits.

7

The Province of Pennsylvania

The Province of Pennsylvania was chartered on March 4, 1681, to William Penn. It seems that the crown of England had owed Sir William Penn, William Penn's father, 16,000 pounds sterling and instead of the actual money, King Charles II offered him a land grant. In fact, even to this day we Pennsylvanians celebrate Charter Day by having various state museums and parks open free of charge for the public to visit.

The fact that the Province of Pennsylvania was directly under British rule helped push the colonists to rebel more quickly than in some other provinces. It's no wonder that many of the key figures in starting the American Revolution were from Pennsylvania.

People like Ben Franklin, Anthony Wayne, and Thomas Paine all made Pennsylvania their home just before the Revolutionary War started. With all the famous people and places like The Valley Forge Encampment and The Brandywine Battlefield, just to name a few, there are definitely a wide variety of places with supernatural phenomena in Pennsylvania.

The Headless Horseman of...Paoli?

The Paoli Massacre was one of the most humiliating events during the Revolutionary War for the Continental Army. Paoli is a small town in Chester County, not far from Valley Forge and the home of one of the most famous generals, aside from George Washington: General "Mad Anthony" Wayne.

Remember Paoli!

One of many rally cries during the Revolutionary War. *Courtesy of Cindy Wolf*

On the night of September 20, 1777, General Wayne's troops were camped in a field in Paoli and were bedded down for the night when, about midnight, a silent force of Redcoats attacked the unsuspecting soldiers as they slept. Using what we would consider today as guerrilla warfare, the British troops were ordered not to use their muskets in the initial assault. Using only knives, swords, or bayonets, they surprised the sleeping Continental Army and killed about fifty-three of them at the outset of the battle without taking any significant losses themselves.

After the battle, about 300 Patriots were wounded and the British only had four casualties. General Wayne was taken to task by his superiors for encamping so close to the British lines. He felt humiliated as well, and took full responsibility for the disaster. He eventually requested a court marshal for himself and was cleared

At least the Headless Horseman's comrades get to rest in peace here.
Courtesy of Cindy Wolf

of all charges. But the fact remains, that the colonials had taken a beating. One they wouldn't soon forget.

Nowadays, the Paoli Massacre is remembered via two monuments. One, the original monument is now so worn down that you can barely read the inscription on it. It was erected in 1817 and has worn down over the decades since its placement. The white obelisk sits in a small brick walled enclosure that also houses the buried remains of those fifty-three unfortunate colonial soldiers who died at the hands of the silently attacking British.

But the other monument, a larger black one, sits out in the open across from a baseball diamond and a walking path surrounded by swing sets and jungle gyms. It really does seem out of place in a public park and no one seems that interested in what it has to say, let alone what it stands for. You don't see many people visiting it and probably most people don't even think twice about it. There are no signs directing you to it and if there had been a victory there for the colonials, we might have a more impressive monument and flocks of people visiting the site.

But is our Headless Horseman, one of the fifty-three fallen soldiers... in a word, no. He does have to do with the Paoli Massacre though and in a very important way.

When my wife and I visited the public Park where the monuments are placed, you'd hardly expect to see a ghostly headless spectre roaming the area. It's tucked away in a rural housing development and surrounded by schools and businesses and of course the things that go with a public park: picnic areas and open fields for playing ball and tossing Frisbees.

According to the legend, one of General Wayne's soldiers actually had a home in the area where they were camping. In order to help save rations, the soldier was allowed to go home every night after he had performed his duties and eat supper with his wife and family, and then sleep and report for duty first thing in the morning. This arrangement worked out well for everybody involved.

On the night of September 20th, the soldier rode his horse home as he usually did. It being late summer, it was probably a pleasant ride through the lush Pennsylvania farmland. That night, as he settled down to sleep, he couldn't shake the feeling that something was terribly, terribly wrong back at the encampment. When he finally managed to get to sleep he had a nightmare that the camp was being attacked by the Redcoats. Waking up in a cold sweat, he hurriedly dressed and prepared to return to the encampment despite his wife pleading for him to wait until daylight when he was supposed to return to camp. He'd had a feeling of dread that

The new monument to those fallen at the Paoli Massacre. *Courtesy of Cindy Wolf*

he'd never experienced before in his life. Somehow he knew his comrades were in mortal peril. Despite his wife's pleas for him to stay with her, he quickly saddled his horse and rode down the darkened road, the pale light of the moon his only guide.

Upon arriving at the encampment his eyes beheld a horrible sight. Burning tents, the stench of death and the screams of agony from his fallen comrades greeted him. Before he could get his bearings he was rushed upon by the Redcoats who promptly took him by surprise. The last sight he saw in his mortal life was the vicious descent of a British soldier's sword arcing towards his unprotected head! Ah, but the story of this unfortunate American patriot doesn't end there.

The locals around the Paoli Massacre site have witnessed over the years a reoccurring paranormal presence that they claim is the guilty, headless spirit of that patriot. Who feels compelled to ride the back roads of Chester County in penance for not being at the camp when his fellow soldiers were being massacred by the British that fateful September night.

You can be sure it's the horseman's spirit by two strange phenomena that accompany an encounter with him. One of these is that the horse's hooves make no sound whatsoever on whatever surface they encounter, be it highway or field. The second thing is that even though he's known as a headless horseman spirit, he still may actually have his head on his shoulders when you first encounter him. But a word of warning: Don't catch his attention! Never make eye contact with this sad spirit; if you do, he may close in on you and tear off his head and present it to you with outstretched arms, and his glaring eyes burning into yours if this should happen, mores the pity for you.

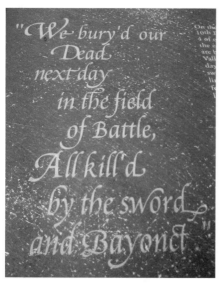

Start making a last will and testament because you're going to need it within a year. They say, who ever the ghost presents his head to will die a violent death within a year of meeting this tragic specter. So be warned. Think twice before setting out on a ghost hunt for this spirit. It might cost you more than a sleepless night.

It's a shame one of them can't rest in peace. *Courtesy of Cindy Wolf*

Sandy Flash:
The Ghostly Rogue of Kennett Square

There were many opportunists that operated in the fledgling colonies of the Americas. Some made their claim to fame as pirates and privateers along the Atlantic coastline. Other would-be rogues were decidedly land locked and plied their own type of piracy along the hills and valleys of the wilderness of the new land. Of these land pirates or highway robbers was a man known to the local Pennsylvanians as Sandy Flash.

Sandy Flash, also known as James Fitzpatrick, was a native of West Marlborough Township. He was a skilled blacksmith by trade, but decided to turn his back on a lawful occupation and instead embarked on a life of crime.

By all accounts, Fitzpatrick was a healthy, husky man, with long, sandy blond hair and a boisterous manner. He was known to blow through his home town of Doe Run riding a sleek horse at top speed earning him the nickname "Sandy Flash." Not satisfied with being a simple blacksmith, Sandy Flash decided to join the Continental Army when the Revolutionary War began. Probably not because he believed in the cause of freedom, but he probably thought he could make a good fortune in war booty and in pillaging the countryside, even though it was his friends and neighbors he'd be robbing.

He fought bravely and was even wounded in 1777. He mustered in as a member of a "flying Camp" and they soon were stationed in New York State. He hated the military rigmarole and was insubordinate on a number of occasions. Finally fed up, he jumped into the Hudson River and swam away from his post. He was eventually caught and flogged as discipline for desertion, but that didn't stop Sandy Flash for a second.

He must've been the equivalent of Harry Houdini as an escape artist, because he escaped from the military prison not once, not twice, but five times! In his final escape, he made his way across the countryside of Chester County and had a change of heart. He thought that the grass was greener on the other side of the fence and promptly joined the army again. Only this time it was the British Army! Because of his ill treatment at the hands of the Continental Army, he decided to join the enemy. He offered his services as a scout and even helped the British in

Kennett Square, Pennsylvania, the ghostly stomping ground of Sandy Flash.
Courtesy of Cindy Wolf

that capacity during the Battle of Brandywine in Chester County. When the Redcoats had to retreat from the area, Sandy Flash had no desire to leave with them. This area was his home. The problem was too many people knew his face and that he'd worked for the British. No one wanted to associate with him, and so, like many other Tories, he was a man without a country.

Sandy Flash decided to do what he did best. He donned several different disguises and became a highway robber plying his trade over much of Southcentral Pennsylvania. Some historians paint him as a man wronged by the Continental Army.

During this phase of his life, he was almost regarded as a Robin Hood type of persona. At least he was by the loyalists who lived in the area. It was said that he never robbed the poor and that he actually went out of his way to help women in distress, and on at least one occasion escorted an old peddler woman along the Chester Pike to Philadelphia and gave her a few extra gold coins for her to buy more merchandise.

As much as the locals didn't like him raiding their homes and farms, the Continental Army had a bone to pick with Sandy Flash and they offered a bounty for his capture. Eventually, he was caught and imprisoned on August 22, 1778.

Not learning from their previous mistake, the army almost allowed him to escape from the prison in Chester County. They then moved him to a more challenging prison that was thought to have been able to hold him, but Sandy Flash proved them wrong once again and managed to almost escape two more times.

A month after his capture, he was executed in the public Square at the corner of Providence and Edgemont streets in the City of Chester. But even then, fate wasn't done with Sandy Flash. He had one more daring escape from the hangman's noose.

When he was placed for his hanging on top of a wagon, the executioner, most likely the sheriff, misjudged the size of the rope and cut it too long. When Sandy Flash was pushed off the edge of the wagon his tiptoes were able to hold up his body weight and kept him from strangling slowly. To remedy the situation, the executioner actually had to climb onto Sandy Flash's broad shoulders and add his extra weight to finish the job of execution. As much as he had some daring escapes in his life, Sandy Flash couldn't escape death...or could he?

Throughout Chester County, there have been numerous sightings over the years of a ghostly figure dashing through towns, such as Kennett Square and Newtown Square, that oddly match the description of Sandy Flash. Perhaps he's still searching for some of the loot he supposedly buried that was never found.

According to different sources, Sandy Flash had a hideout near Castle Rock, Pennsylvania. Supposedly, it was cave hidden near a creek in a farmstead near a bend on the road. This treasure has never been found. In the 1950s and 60s, people in the area used to look for it so often that the local authorities thought it was becoming a hazard, so they blocked up the cave and hid the entrance. Perhaps the spirit of Sandy Flash is also looking for the cave on his nightly rides.

Another location that the spirit of Sandy Flash is known to have manifested is in an old Tavern in Newtown Square. Not surprising since this was the scene of one of his last known robberies before he was caught and executed in Chester.

If you happen to be on the road between Kennett Square and Newtown Square and you see a figure riding on horseback, keep an eye on his destination. You might just find a financial windfall of the paranormal kind.

The Battle of Brandywine

9/11. Everyone who hears that date automatically thinks of the terrorist attacks on the World Trade Center, Flight 93, and the Pentagon, and they'd be right to do so. But, 2001 isn't the only 9/11 that was a dark, sad day in American history. September 11, 1777 was also a day of an attack on America by a foreign enemy.

During the Revolutionary War, the British army was advancing towards Philadelphia, Pennsylvania, the newly formed capital of America. On September 10, 1777, General George Washington placed Continental Army troops at Brandywine, in Chadds Ford, Pennsylvania, to stop the British advance. He placed them there because of the high ground. (It was always a good military tactic to take the high ground when facing the enemy.) But Washington hadn't counted on one unpredictable thing: the weather. On September 11, 1777, the morning was covered in a thick, ground fog. This proved advantageous for the British, who used it to outmaneuver Washington's well-placed troops. Due in part to some poor scouting

A view of Washington's Headquarters that a soldier from the battle might have seen. *Courtesy of Cindy Wolf*

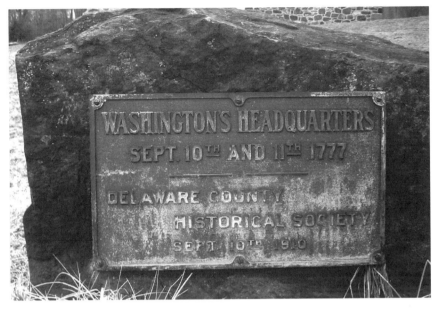

A very sad day for the Continental Army, which is why their spirits linger here.
Courtesy of Cindy Wolf

reports, the Continental Army was surprised and outflanked by the British. Washington's troops did their best, and by all accounts fought valiantly, but when the day was done, they had been forced to retreat back to the town of Chester, Pennsylvania. The British had definitely won at Brandywine on September 11, 1777.

Today, the Brandywine Battlefield is a public historical site and is operated by The Pennsylvania Historical and Museum Commission. The aftermath of the battle has generated tales of spectral Revolutionary War soldiers that, at times, re-enact the battle fought there so long ago.

My wife, Cindy, and I visited the Battlefield, and although we didn't have any paranormal encounters, I felt there was a strange feel to the grounds. I'm not one for getting psychic impressions and most of the time, as most people will tell you, I'm about as psychic as a cement block, but I could definitely feel some kind of presence at Brandywine. There weren't too many visitors at the Battlefield that day and we had most of it and the few surrounding stone buildings to ourselves. As we wandered around the peaceful rolling hills and observed the old stone building that was George Washington's Headquarters, I just could not shake that weird vibe. We had brought our dog, Toby, with us and he seemed interested in certain places at

The front view of Washington's Brandywine Headquarters. *Courtesy of Cindy Wolf*

the battlefield, almost as if he were drawn to them. Looking back, I didn't think of it at the time, but its entirely possible that he was picking up on the same weird, paranormal vibes that I was.

This location had been a solid defeat for the Continental Army and emotions had to be running high. As in most places where a traumatic event has occurred there is usually some sort of psychic imprint. Gettysburg is a good example. What people may have experienced here over the years is probably a residual haunting. Most accounts of paranormal activity seem to be cases where the soldiers' spirits are acting out the Battle. One exception to this is the appearance of spirit of "Mad Anthony" Wayne. His ghost has been sighted riding around on his horse, Nab.

As we left the Brandywine Battlefield, I had the distinct feeling that there was something more here than met the eye. We might not have had much luck in sighting anything paranormal because of the time of year we visited. The battle took place at the end of summer; we were there at the beginning of spring. Perhaps, I might just go back again in September.

The Delaware Colony

The Delaware colony has had a variety of founders ranging all the way back to sixteenth century when it was first discovered by the Spanish and Portuguese. Even the famous Dutch explorer, Henry Hudson, who is more widely known in exploring New York, had a hand in exploring the Delaware Bay.

The Delaware colony not only declared its independence from the British crown in 1776 along with the other colonies, since Delaware was also governed by the Commonwealth or Pennsylvania, they declared independence from Pennsylvania as well. When they

Many a colonial spirit has tread this cobblestone path. *Courtesy of Cindy Wolf*

separated from Pennsylvania in order to make certain there would be no territorial disputes, the government of Delaware employed Charles Mason and Jeremiah Dixon, (yes, the same Mason and Dixon, who are famous for creating the Mason Dixon line that separates the north from the south) to officially name the state boundary.

When the Revolutionary War broke out, 4,000 men enlisted in the Militia, but the only engagement ever fought during the Revolutionary War in Delaware was at a place called, "Cooche's Bridge," near Newark, Delaware. Even though Delaware doesn't have the number of battlefields as other colonies, such as New York and Massachusetts, there's no shortage of haunted locations. No other colony can lay claim to its very own Were-fox, a wine-sipping specter, or a ghost writer.

The Wine-sipping Spectre of Woodburn

Woodburn Mansion is the current home of the Governor of Delaware. Originally, the house wasn't built for the Governor's home. It was built in 1790 by a Revolutionary War general by the name of Charles Hillyard.

Over the years, at least four spirits have manifested themselves on a regular basis in Woodburn. Two of those four spirits are from the time of the Revolutionary War era. In the years before Woodburn became the Governor's home, many guests had sighted spirits here.

One of the first hauntings was recorded in 1805 by a man named Lorenzo Dow. Dow was a Methodist minister who was visiting the mansion. One night, while getting ready to retire to his room for the night, he encountered what he called an elderly-looking stranger upstairs near the fireplace. He told the wife of the current owner of Woodburn the next morning what he had seen. She was adamant that there were no other guests, elderly or otherwise, currently staying in the mansion.

Much to her surprise, the wife of the owner also encountered the same elderly apparition not long after minister had seen him. Sixty-five years later, the elderly-looking spirit was still frightening people.

Another house guest in the 1870s almost died of fright when he encountered the old colonial gentleman's spirit sitting next to the upstairs fireplace. The man was so frightened by the apparition that he actually fainted on the spot and other household members had to summon a nearby doctor from Dover to revive the poor man.

Woodburn Mansion, home of the spirit with a drinking problem.
Courtesy of Cindy Wolf

Some people have speculated over the years that this elderly ghost is none other than Charles Hillyard, the original builder of Woodburn. He survived the Revolutionary War and had obtained the rank of Colonel, but eventually death takes us all and Charles Hillyard died at an elderly age in the mansion he built and dearly was attached to in life. He must have loved spending time sitting next to the fireplace so much that he's come back from his eternal rest or perhaps resting by the fireplace is his way of resting in piece. To each his own afterlife...

Another colonial spirit has a unique way of making its presence known at Woodburn. This particular spirit has a problem. A drinking problem to be exact. An apparition dressed in a gentleman's powdered wig and colonial-style clothing has been seen many times by guests and residents of Woodburn. He's usually spotted in the dining room sitting on a chair and sipping a glass of wine. According to the first governor to live in Woodburn, Charles Terry, Jr., the alcoholic spirit has been known to drain several bottles of fine wine from the wine cellar in the space of one evening. In fact, one of the employees of the governor actually witnessed the ghost draining one of the decanters of wine from the dining room.

Rumor has it, that before Woodburn became the official governor's mansion, the servants of the former owner would place full decanters of wine on the table in the dining room overnight to placate the wine-loving spirit. These decanters would always be drained by the next morning.

You almost have to wonder: Do they need to call in an exorcist or start a twelve-step program to stop the spirit from draining the wine cellar?

Woodburn Mansion also served as a Revolutionary War hospital and a Colonel who died there is known to walk about the manor and grounds on certain nights. So it would seem that whatever spirits reside at Woodburn, one thing is for certain: They still do in death what they loved doing in life.

The Werefox of Brandywine Creek

A short drive from Wilmington, Delaware, is the Brandywine Creek State Park. It sits right on the Pennsylvania border and is right off Route 202. There are two entrances to the park and if you're interested in looking for the elusive werefox of Brandywine Creek, you'll want to seek out the lower entrance near the bridge to start your search.

If you're extremely lucky, you might catch a glimpse of a werefox here.
Courtesy of Cindy Wolf

This particular werefox is also named Red Dog Fox by the locals and in the eighteenth century during the Revolutionary War, this werefox had a human name and identity. He was known as Gil Thoreau. Gil was a teenager, or at least looked like he was in his teens during the war. You'll see why I mention this later. His father was reputed to have worked for General Lafayette, and Gil himself was supposed to have done scouting missions for the Continental Army.

Gil isn't the first werefox in existence, though, and while werewolves may be more widely known, werefoxes have been known to originate in ancient oriental mythology and they differ somewhat from their wolf counterparts. In Chinese and Japanese mythology, werefoxes are almost always female. Although there *are* some cases of them being male, there are far more female werefoxes. According to Japanese lore, a fox who has reached the age of 500 years has the ability to take on a human form. Werefoxes have several weaknesses and one of them is that they will revert back to their fox form when asleep.

Another weakness is that even though they can assume human form, they still retains their tails. Perhaps that's why by certain accounts Gil Thoreau never liked being in towns and kept to the woodlands. Was he afraid of being pegged as a supernatural creature?

In any case, I'm sure that his alleged ability to change into a large fox was a great help to him when going on scouting missions for the Continental Army. Gil Thoreau has been spotted in his fox form slinking along the banks of the Brandywine Creek.

My wife and I, when we visited the area, had no luck in spotting any wildlife, let alone a large, red fox. That by no means says that the spirit of Gil Thoreau doesn't exist. It just means that we had no luck in spotting him.

The creek is the central feature of the park. Many people use the park for hiking, canoeing, and fishing. Looking out from the creek bank, its plain to see how easy it would be for a skilled woodsman to scout the area. A scout in shape-shifted fox form would be even harder to spot. Evidently, Gil Thoreau was a successful scout and had evaded capture. He was supposed to have lived until the age of 45. Local people living when he died claimed that he still had the appearance of a teenager at the time of his alleged death.

So here's the question. Did Gil Thoreau really die at the age of 45 or did he just assume the form of Red Dog Fox and disappear into the wilderness? Sightings of the werefox have been recorded from Brandywine Creek to as far north as Watertown, New York.

The next time you're walking along the Brandywine Creek and you see some rustling in the underbrush, maybe...just maybe... it might be Gil Thoreau going about his business.

The Ghostwriter of Dickinson Mansion

Just off Kitts Hummock Road, about seven miles southeast of Dover, Delaware, lies Dickinson Mansion. This is the homestead and plantation of John Dickinson, who has been nicknamed, "The Penman of the Revolution."

John Dickinson was most well known in his time for writing many essays supporting the fight for American independence. Some people claim that his patriotic spirit is still writing at his home to this day.

My wife, Cindy, and I visited Dickinson Mansion on a Saturday afternoon in June near closing time. It's not as if I had planned to arrive so close to their closing time but there was a considerable amount of road construction going on the main route and I had taken a wrong turn and had to backtrack to the mansion on a back road. It turns out, the construction actually helped our visit that day. There were no other tourists there to visit the mansion because of the construction and the lateness of the day. We were fortunate enough to get a private tour of the grounds and the inside of the mansion.

Once we parked in the lot across from a small barn-like building that was the Visitors Center, we found a man dressed in colonial garb. He directed us to the main house for the last tour of the day. Since it was close to closing time, we were given a somewhat whirlwind tour of the house but, that in my mind was better than getting no tour at all. Besides, how could we pass up getting a private free tour?

We walked up the long cobblestone sidewalk that led towards the mansion; on our way we passed the stone enclosed grave site of Samuel Dickinson, John Dickinson's father, who had built the mansion and plantation.

Once we reached the mansion, we walked around the corner and up to a wooden staircase that ended at an imposing, pale green door, with a large brass knocker. Naturally, I used the door knocker which turned out to be heavier than I thought and it boomed against the door. It promptly opened and we were greeted by a woman also dressed in colonial garb who was to be our guide.

Cindy was in charge of taking pictures. For as long as we've been together, she's always had more luck at capturing paranormal pictures than I've ever had.

Dickinson Mansion, haunt of a literal "Ghost" writer. *Courtesy of Cindy Wolf*

As we walked through the various rooms in the mansion, the parlor, the dining room, upstairs bedrooms, we listened to our guide describe what was considered to be typical daily life in the Dickinson household back in the eighteenth century.

We finally made our way down to the cellar and, to my surprise, the kitchen. The kitchen was built on the lower level for some reason. I've been to a lot of colonial-style buildings researching this and other books and this is the first time I had actually seen something like this. Not only was the kitchen in the cellar, but there was also a storage area and a workroom for the mansion servants down on the cellar level as well. At this point of the tour the historical guide asked us if we had any questions about the mansion. Boy! Did I ever!

This is usually my cue to ask if there are any tales or stories of hauntings and I wasn't disappointed in her answer. Without looking the least bit surprised at my question, our guide told us that we weren't the first people to ask her that question.

Other guides had also been asked that question and although those guides have had experiences in the mansion, she herself had not, but she could show us where the other people had seen and heard some strange things over the years.

With a clear idea of why we were there, she could now give us a truly unique tour of the haunted areas of the mansion. Heading

The spirit of John Dickinson likes to take afternoon naps in this room.
Courtesy of Cindy Wolf

back upstairs, the first room she showed us was one of the children's upstairs bedrooms.

It looked to be a boy's room. Scattered on the floor, under the rope bed, was a collection of tin soldiers. According to our guide, these soldiers would change position on their own overnight when no one was in the mansion. A guide would close and lock up for the night and the soldiers would be in their place, the next morning the opening guide would find them scattered all over the room with no rational explanation as to how they were moved during the night.

The next room she took us to was the master bedroom. It was furnished in colonial style with a table, large four-post canopy bed and something a little creepy and extra: the wax figure of a manservant holding a towel over a washbasin.

In this room, our tour guide explained many visitors have commented on how the bed always looks like it was just slept in. Adds a bit of authenticity right? The problem is that the employees and guides are supposed to keep the bed made up. They're not supposed to make it seem as though someone had been sleeping. No one has been able to explain why this happens all the time.

Most of the guides feel as though it's the spirit of John Dickinson taking his usual afternoon nap. Now if I were on one of those ghost hunting shows, this is a spot I'd definitely be setting up those infrared digital camcorders to record all night.

According to our guide, other paranormal investigators have picked up EVPs (Electronic Voice Phenomena) of the sound of a quill pen scratching on parchment, as well as other noises, such as the sound of footsteps and doors opening and closing.

After thanking our guide for the special tour, we decided to check Cindy's digital camera for any evidence of the paranormal. The only picture that I could plainly see an orb was the one taken in the servant's workroom in the cellar. Cindy and I both agreed that the trip to Dickinson Mansion was worth our time.

Cooche's Bridge

The one and only battle fought during the Revolutionary War in Delaware occurred near Newark and was fought near a place called Cooche's Bridge on September 3, 1777. Aside from being haunted, Cooche's Bridge has one other claim to fame. It's supposedly where the Stars and Stripes, our nation's flag, sewn by Betsy Ross, was first held aloft in a battle.

The Cooche's Bridge battle actually started before September 3rd. On August 30th, British Generals Cornwallis, Howe, and a Hessian General Knyphausen moved their forces into the Wilmington area.

The colonial army under George Washington moved on them in a series of guerrilla warfare attacks that they had learned from the local Native Americans. Finally, several days later, the Redcoats and

The battle of Cooche's Bridge took place near here. *Courtesy of Cindy Wolf*

their allies the Hessians made several charges in retaliation in the area of Cooche's Bridge, but they were repelled by the determined Continental Army.

Unfortunately, the colonial militia's victory was short lived and because of running out of ammunition they were forced to retreat from Cooche's Bridge. All in all, it was a relatively small battle in the war of independence and there were only a few casualties on either side of the fighting.

One ghostly legend says that during the battle, a British soldier had his head shot cleanly off and his headless spirit now wanders the back roads between Wilmington and Newark on foggy moonless nights searching for his lost appendage.

He must be having a tough time of it in any case. When we decided to search out Cooche's Bridge to research this story, I had a hard enough time finding the location of where the battle took place. In fact, I'm not sure I actually *did* find it. There's a road off the Old Baltimore Pike that's listed on our map and GPS as Olde Cooche's Bridge Road. Even armed with modern navigation technology we still had a hard time finding the bridge. We drove up and down the length of Olde Cooche's Bridge Road and all we could find at either end of the road was a dead end. There was a small stone bridge on the southern side of the road near the sign for Cooche's Bridge

Could this be where a headless Redcoat walks on foggy nights? *Courtesy of Cindy Wolf*

Road. Lacking any better prospects, we decided that this must be the bridge that they were talking about.

All I can say is that if this is where the battle took place, no wonder the headless ghost of the British soldier is still looking for his head after all this time. It was hard enough for us to find it in the daytime with our heads still attached.

Paranormal Profile:
The Immortal George Washington

NAME: *Washington, George*
BORN: *February 22, 1732*
DIED: *December 14, 1799*

"First in war, first in peace, and first in the hearts of his countrymen, he was second to none in humble and enduring scenes of private life."

~Henry "Light Horse Harry" Lee

George Washington, the man who would someday lead our fledgling country into battle against the British, and who would forever be known as the "Father of Our Country" was born on February 22, 1732, on his family's Pope Creek Estate, in Westmoreland County, Virginia.

Who would've ever suspected that the boy who could not tell a lie, would have grown into the legend he is today. Not only has George Washington's life become the stuff of legends, but his afterlife is just as amazing.

In his teenage years, George Washington worked as a surveyor of rural land in his home province of Virginia. When he wasn't even out of his teens, he acquired his first public office: Surveyor of Culpepper County. This early career served him later in life as Commander of the Continental Army. Having familiarized himself with the local terrain gave him invaluable knowledge that would later prove very useful in the Revolutionary War.

During this early era of his life, young George was introduced to the Ohio Company by his half-brother, Lawrence Washington. The Ohio Company was trying to colonize the land west of Pittsburgh, and Lawrence Washington was the Adjutant of the colony.

After Lawrence's untimely death in 1752, George Washington, barely twenty years old, took over his half-brother's position of

Courtesy of Christopher E. Wolf

Colonial Adjutant and effectively ended up joining the British army as a Major.

Three years later, Major Washington joined British General Edward Braddock's ill-fated military campaign to reclaim the Ohio colony they had been forced out of a year earlier by the French and Native Americans.

The campaign proved unsuccessful (General Braddock was killed). Major Washington distinguished himself in battle and spawned a few legends, (legends we'll examine later) among the Native Americans who had faced him in battle.

It wasn't until three years later, when he joined the Forbes expedition, that the British troops finally managed to drive out the French from what was then known as Fort Duquesne and later as Fort Pitt.

Tired of the military life, George Washington retired from active duty and settled down for a peaceful life as a plantation owner. For the next sixteen years, he led a civilian life and dabbled in politics only in his home province of Virginia.

A year into his retirement, he met wealthy widow, Martha Dandridge Custus, and after a whirlwind courtship and engagement (lasting a whole three weeks), George Washington asked her to marry him, and she said yes.

Their marriage was a good one, and the newlyweds moved to Mount Vernon Plantation, where they led peaceful lives. Life was looking rather good to George Washington. By 1775, Mount Vernon Plantation had doubled in size. George was a respected military hero of the French and Indian wars, and was a large land owner to boot. Throughout his civilian years, Washington had always taken a leading role in growing colonial resistance to British rule. As a local politician, he attended the first Virginia convention and was selected to be their delegate to the first Continental Congress in Philadelphia.

When hostilities broke out in New England in 1775, George Washington knew the time for action was at hand. He arrived at the second Continental Congress in full military dress uniform to show them that he was ready to fight for his freedom and for America.

The Congress wasted no time in creating a Continental Army and the very next day, on the nomination of John Adams, George Washington was sworn in as Commander-in-Chief. History books are full of information about General George Washington's war exploits.

From his early success in driving the British out of Boston, to his lowest moments at Valley Forge in the winter of 1777, and his final victory in 1781 in Yorktown, no one can deny that this man was one of the deciding influences in our nation's fight for independence and freedom.

After the war ended, Washington retired once again to Mount Vernon. His retirement was short lived, to say the least. A mere four years into this well-earned retirement, he was persuaded to attend the Constitutional Convention in Philadelphia in 1787, where he was unanimously elected the Convention President.

Two years later, George Washington was again unanimously elected, only this time as the first President of the United States of America on April 30, 1789. John Adams was his Vice President. Washington really didn't want the responsibility of being President, but he took the role seriously and made sure that the office never mimicked European Royal Courts. In fact, he refused to be called, "Your Excellency," and preferred the title, "Mr. President."

George Washington proved he could lead the nation in peacetime as well as in wartime, and when the time came for his re-election, he was unanimously voted in. Something no other president in history has ever achieved since.

George could've had third term in office if he had wanted it, but he wanted no third term and its because of his wishes that no president can serve three consecutive terms of office. Washington retired from politics in 1797 and was happy to return to Mount Vernon.

Two years later, on December 12, 1799, Washington was inspecting his property during a freezing rainstorm and caught a bad case of pneumonia. A day later, George Washington, the Father of Our Country, uttered his last words: "Tis' well," and then passed away.

George Washington's body may have expired, but his spirit still lives on. His ghost has been seen in almost as many places as he's been reported to have slept in during the Revolutionary War. Now let's take a closer look at a few of the legends and supernatural tales that have surrounded the Father of Our Country.

WASHINGTON'S GHOST
AT VALLEY FORGE

Almost everyone in the world has heard of the saying: "It's like Washington at Valley Forge.." They're usually complaining about some hardship that is happening in their life at that moment and comparing it to the hardship that the Continental Army endured at the winter encampment at Valley forge, Pennsylvania, in 1777 during the Revolutionary War.

But what was Washington and the army doing there? And was it really as bad as they say it was? Most importantly, (to us anyway), does the ghost of George Washington and his army still haunt the area today? Answers to those questions and more, was what I wanted to find out.

To get firsthand information for this book, my wife, Cindy and I took a short drive from our house to visit the Valley Forge National Historical Park. As much of a history buff that I am, Cindy was shocked by my revelation that I had never been to Valley Forge before today. I've made hundreds of trips to Gettysburg, but I just never thought of going to Valley Forge.

It was a very easy drive, and once we had parked in the public lot, it was short walk to the Welcome Center to get an overview of Valley Forge. I was hoping to get some leads on ghost sightings from some

The specters of the Continental Army roam these huts at night. *Courtesy of Cindy Wolf*

of the park rangers, but I didn't really expect to, because as course of policy they usually play down anything other than the historic aspects of the National Park.

First though, I wanted to understand what had taken place here in the winter of 1777. It turns out I had a lot learn. The first thing I wanted to know was why did George Washington camp the Continental Army here? I mean, why not further south in Virginia or South Carolina where it was warmer for the winter?

Well, it seems as though he didn't have any better choice, because, you see, the British army under Sir William Howe was dead set on capturing the city of Philadelphia. Why? Because unlike nowadays, back then, Philadelphia and not Washington, D.C., was the capital of the nation.

When the Redcoats landed at Head of Elk on the Chesapeake Bay, they swiftly made a beeline for Philadelphia and Pennsylvania.

General Washington and the Continental Army tried to stop them twice. Once at the Battle of Brandywine and once at the Battle of Germantown, but the British defeated them both times and continued to move to Philly and managed to capture it. What good it did them is debatable.

To keep the British from gaining more access to inland towns in Pennsylvania, Washington had his army encamp at Valley

Forge, to bottle the British in. That's why they set up camp there.

Another reason for the encampment was that Washington realized that as good as his men were at fighting the British, they could do better. Washington knew they needed more formal military training so he arranged to have a German by the name of Baron Von Steuben teach his men proper military maneuvers so they could more effectively fight the Redcoats. They would get both this training and stop the British by camping at Valley Forge.

We left the Welcome Center and caught one of the free shuttle buses over to the park. These shuttles circle the park and you can catch one at several different stops about every ten minutes. It's great service, but hardly anyone seemed to be using it as there were only a few people on the bus besides us. I wanted to see the encampment for myself and the bus would also eventually take us to the main site I was interested in visiting that day: Washington's Headquarters.

Our first stop in the Valley Forge Park was at a series of small wooden huts built out of rough hewn logs called "redoubts" at the outer line defense. This is where General Peter Muhlenberg's troops formed the first line of defense for the Continental Army. As I walked over to listen to two Revolutionary War re-enactors dressed as American Militiamen talking about life as a soldier in the Continental

Is this redoubt haunted by one of General Muhlenburg's soldiers? *Courtesy of Cindy Wolf*

The officers didn't have much more luxury within their quarters than the enlisted men. *Courtesy of Cindy Wolf*

Army, Cindy wandered among the half a dozen or so log huts to take pictures of the inside and outside of the dwellings in hopes of getting some orbs or ectoplasm.

After listening to the Militia men for a few minutes, I found Cindy and had a look for myself at some of the huts. It was definitely enlightening, and the huts showed how rough living conditions were for the soldiers at Valley Forge that winter.

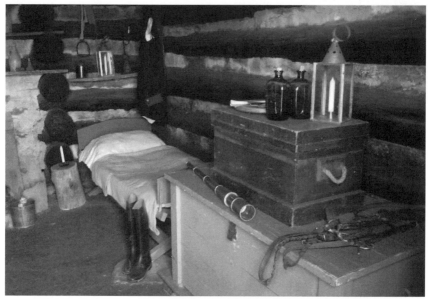

As a medieval period re-enactor, years ago I had some experience with primitive camping, to look at these huts and see the muddy floors and furnishings, (the huts that had them), I wouldn't have wanted to camp in them in the summertime, let alone be stuck in them during a harsh Pennsylvania winter.

Our next stop took us to the National Memorial Arch, which is dedicated to the soldiers who wintered at Valley Forge in 1777-78.

Cindy took a few pictures of the arch and it truly is impressive. I'm not sure what the gargoyle faces are supposed to represent though.

On our journey to Washington's Headquarters we stopped to get a few pictures of General "Mad Anthony" Wayne's statue. If you

Soldiers' spirits have been seen congregating around this monument.
Courtesy of Cindy Wolf

read the previous Paranormal Profile on him, you'll agree that he was quite a controversial hero.

According to Dennis William Hauck's book, *The National Directory of Haunted Places*, the ghost of General Wayne has been spotted riding his horse, Nab, around the statue. Sad to say, we saw no sign of the mad general, or his horse. The only thing we spotted were a large amount of deer grazing in Wayne's Woods nearby. Better luck next time.

After walking back to the shuttle stop. We boarded the next available bus a few minutes later and we were finally on our way to the place I really wanted to visit: The Isaac Potts House, where George Washington had made his headquarters.

Our old friend, "Mad Anthony," has been known to make a ghostly ride around his statue at Valley Forge. *Courtesy of Christopher E. Wolf*

Even without ghosts, this face is enough to frighten you in the dark.
Courtesy of Cindy Wolf

In order to get to the headquarters you have to walk a short path, where you'll be greeted by a park ranger who will wait for a small group to form before leading you to Washington's Headquarters. There were maybe a dozen people or so – people in our group included two women who seemed very interested in possible hauntings and ghosts at Valley Forge. They asked the ranger about ghosts before I had a chance to myself. Fortunately, we were lucky enough to get a ranger who had some personal knowledge of the supernatural surrounding Valley Forge.

He told the ladies that as far as he knew there weren't any Revolutionary War ghosts haunting the Valley Forge park, but he did mention that there was supposedly some kind of entity haunting the Valley Forge Railroad Station and it was presumed to be from the nineteenth rather than eighteenth century.

Interestingly, though, my research uncovered that the spirit of Baron Von Steuben, the man George Washington hired to train the Continental Army at Valley Forge, was seen along the Schuylkill River, near the old Valley Forge Railroad Station that we were standing in front at that moment.

We then moved on to Washington's Headquarters, which was just down a long cement staircase. As we walked, the ranger explained more about the location.

Once we were inside the old stone house, Cindy went upstairs to try and capture some paranormal photos while I stayed downstairs

The ghost of Baron Von Steuben has been seen along these railroad tracks.
Courtesy of Cindy Wolf

In this house, George Washington had a fateful vision. *Courtesy of Cindy Wolf*

and talked to the ranger. My only question for him was about an incident I had read about George Washington having a vision about the future that was given to him by a spirit at Valley Forge. I asked the Ranger if he knew anything about the legend. I was in luck.

Not only did the ranger know about it, he showed me the exact room and fireplace where it happened back in 1777. This was fantastic! As soon as Cindy returned from the upstairs, I wanted her to take some pictures of this room and fireplace.

It turns out she had a surprise of her own for me. While she was taking a picture of Washington's bedroom, (Yes, he really did sleep here), she had two shots; one was normal, the other had a smoky ectoplasm drifting in front of the bed.

I told her about the room with the fireplace and she took some photos, but she had never heard the story of George Washington's vision and perhaps you haven't either, so I'll retell it as I've heard it. This story has been printed in magazines, newspapers, and even on the Internet, but it was first published in the Civil War veteran's newspaper, *The National Tribune*, which was later renamed *The Stars and Stripes*.

The story goes something like this: George Washington was having serious doubts about whether he and the rest of the Continental Army

This photo was taken just before... *Courtesy of Cindy Wolf*

...this photo was taken. Notice the swirls of ectoplasm. *Courtesy of Cindy Wolf*

Yes, George Washington really did sleep here and possibly still does. *Courtesy of Cindy Wolf*

Could the fate of our nation possibly have changed in this room? *Courtesy of Cindy Wolf*

should continue to fight the Revolutionary War. At Valley Forge, in the winter of 1777, Washington and his men fought one of the toughest adversaries they would ever face...and it wasn't the British. It was their own self doubt.

One day that winter, Washington was as distraught as the rest of his men. But suddenly, he had renewed faith in their chance of victory over the British. What caused this miraculous change of attitude? According to this following newspaper article, originally written by Wesley Bradshaw in *The National Tribune* in December of 1880, this is what happened on that fateful day to George Washington at Valley Forge:

George Washington's Remarkable Vision

The last time I ever saw Anthony Sherman was on July 4, 1859, in Independence Square. He was then 99 years old, and becoming very feeble. But though so old, his dimming eyes rekindled as he gazed upon Independence Hall, which he came to visit once more.

"Let us go into the hall," he said. "I want to tell you of an incident of Washington's life – one which no one alive knows of except myself; and if you live, you will before long, see it verified.

"From the opening of the Revolution we experienced all phases of fortune, now good and now ill; one time victorious and another conquered. The darkest period we had, I think, was when Washington, after several reverses, retreated to Valley Forge, where he resolved to spend the winter of 1777.

"Ah! I have often seen our dear commander's care-worn cheeks as he would be conversing with a confidential officer about the condition of his poor soldiers. You have doubtless heard the story of Washington's going into the thicket to pray. Well, it was not only true, but he used often to pray in secret for aid and comfort from God, the interposition of whose Divine Providence brought us safely through the darkest days of tribulation.

"One day, I remember well, the chilly winds whistled through the leafless trees, though the sky was cloudless and the sun shone brightly, he remained in his quarters nearly all the afternoon alone. When he came out, I noticed that his face was a shade paler than usual, and there seemed to be something on his mind of more than ordinary importance.

"Returning just after dusk, he dispatched an orderly to the quarters of the officer I mentioned who was presently in attendance. After a preliminary conversation of about half an hour, Washington, gazing upon his companion with that strange look of dignity which he alone could command, said to the latter:

'I do not know whether it is owing to anxiety of my mind, or what, but this afternoon, as I was sitting at this table engaged in preparing a dispatch, something seemed to disturb me. Looking up, I beheld standing opposite me a singular beautiful female. So astonished was I, for I had given strict orders not to be disturbed, that it was some moments before I found language to inquire the cause of her presence. A second, a third, and even a fourth time did I repeat my question, but received no answer from my mysterious visitor except a slight raising of her eyes.

'Presently I heard a voice saying, "Son of the Republic, look and learn." 'While at the same time my visitor extended her arm eastwardly. I now beheld a heavy white vapor at some distance rising fold upon fold. This gradually dissipated, and I looked upon a strange scene. Before me lay spread out in one vast plain all the countries of the world – Europe, Asia, Africa, and America. I saw rolling and tossing, between Europe and America, the billows of the Atlantic, and between Asia and America lay the Pacific. "Son of the Republic," 'said the same mysterious voice as before,' "look and learn." 'At that moment, I beheld a dark, shadowy being, like an angel, standing, or rather floating in the hollow air, between Europe and America. Dipping water out of the ocean in the hollow of each hand, he sprinkled some on America with his right hand while his left hand he cast some on Europe. Immediately a cloud raised from these countries and joined in mid-ocean. For a while it remained stationary, and then moved slowly westward, until it enveloped America in its murky folds. Sharp flashes of lightning gleamed through it at intervals, and I heard the smothered groans and cries of the American people.

'A second time the angel dipped water from the ocean, and sprinkled it out as before. The dark cloud was then drawn back to the ocean, in whose heaving bellows it sank from view. A third time I heard the mysterious voice saying, "Son of the Republic, look and learn." 'I cast my eyes upon America and beheld villages and towns and cities springing up one after another until the whole land, from the Atlantic to the Pacific, was dotted with them. Again I heard the mysterious voice say, "Son of the Republic, the end of the century cometh, look and learn."

'At this the dark shadowy angel turned his face southward, and from Africa I saw an ill-omened specter approach our land. It flitted slowly over every town and city of the latter. The inhabitants presently set themselves in battle array against each other. As I continued looking, I saw a bright angel, on whose brow rested a crown of light, on which was traced the word "Union," bearing the American flag which he placed between the divided nation, and said, "Remember ye are brethren." Instantly, the inhabitants casting from them their weapons became friends once more, and united around the National Standard.

'And again I heard the mysterious voice saying, "Son of the Republic, look and learn." At this the dark, shadowy angel placed a trumpet to his mouth and blew three distinct blasts; and taking water from the ocean, he sprinkled it upon Europe, Asia, and Africa.

'Then my eyes beheld a fearful scene. From each of these countries arose thick, black clouds that were soon joined into one. And throughout this mass, there gleamed a dark red light by which I saw hordes of armed men, who moving with the cloud, marched by land and by sea to America, which the country was enveloped in the volume of the cloud. And I dimly saw these vast armies devastate the whole country, and burn the villages, towns and cities that I beheld springing up. As my ears listened to the thundering of the cannon, clashing of swords, and the shouts and cries of millions in mortal combat.

'I again heard the mysterious voice saying, "Son of the Republic, look and learn." When the voice had ceased, the dark shadowy angel placed his trumpet once more to his mouth, and blew a long and fearful blast. Instantly, a light shone down from above me, and pierced and broke into fragments the dark cloud which enveloped America. At the same moment the angel upon whose head still shone the word "Union" and who bore our national flag in one hand and a sword in the other, descended from the heavens attended by legions of white spirits. These immediately joined the inhabitants of America, who I perceived were well-nigh overcome, but who immediately taking courage again closed up their broken ranks and renewed the battle. Again, amid the fearful noise of the conflict, I heard the mysterious voice saying, "Son of the Republic, look and learn."

'As the voice ceased, the shadowy angel for the last time dipped water from the ocean and sprinkled it upon America. Instantly the dark cloud rolled back, together with the armies it had brought, leaving the inhabitants of the land victorious. Then once more I beheld the villages, towns and cities, springing up where I had seen them before, while the bright angel, plating the azure standard he had brought in the midst of them, cried with a loud voice: "While the stars remain, and the heavens send down dew upon the earth, so long shall the Union last." And taking from his brow the crown on which was blazoned the word "Union," he placed it upon the Standard, while the people kneeling down, said, "Amen."

'The scene instantly began to fade and dissolve, and I at last saw nothing but the rising, curling vapor I at first beheld. This also disappearing, I found myself once more gazing upon the mysterious visitor, who in the same voice I had heard before, said, "Son of the Republic, what you have seen is thus interpreted. Three great perils will come upon the Republic. The most fearful is the third." '(The comment on his word, *third* is: "The help against the THIRD peril comes in the shape of Divine assistance; passing which, the whole world united shall not prevail against her. Let every child of the Republic learn to live for his God, his land and Union.")

'With these words the vision vanished, and I started from my seat and felt that I had seen a vision wherein had been shown me the birth, progress and destiny of the United States.'

"Such my friends," concluded the venerable narrator, "were the words I heard from Washington's own lips, and America will do well to profit by them."

Cindy and I both felt it was pretty amazing that we were now standing in the same room that might have very well changed the fate of our nation and most certainly changed the course of George Washington's life.

Cindy captured this crescent orb inside the guard redoubts, outside Washington's Headquarters. *Courtesy of Cindy Wolf*

But our supernatural encounters with Valley Forge weren't over yet. As we were leaving Washington's headquarters, Cindy saw some more redoubts up on a small hill to our right across a small stream and wanted to take some more pictures of the log huts. It turns out it was a good idea.

These redoubts hosted the personal guards of George Washington. One may yet still be at his post. *Courtesy of Cindy Wolf*

These huts were for the men assigned to guard George Washington's safety and in one of the pictures you can see that Cindy captured what looks like an ectoplasmic orb. Was this a ghost of a guard still at his post? It could very well be.

GEORGE WASHINGTON AT...
GETTYSBURG?

If the encampment at Valley Forge in the winter of 1777 was a major turning point in the Revolutionary War, then certainly Gettysburg could be considered the turning point in the Civil War.

If Gettysburg held the key to an eventual Union victory, then one of the most important battles at Gettysburg would be the Battle of Little Round Top on July 2, 1863. But what does this have to do with George Washington? As it turns out, plenty!

On July 1st, the 20th Maine was on its way to take part in the Battle of Gettysburg. As they marched through Maryland towards Pennsylvania the men were weary; they knew their presence was needed and they marched as fast as they could. The tired soldiers trudged on through the night. They realized they were getting close to Gettysburg when they came across a fork in the road. Colonel Joshua Lawrence Chamberlain, the commander of the 20th Maine, was unsure of which road to take and decided to discuss his options with his officers.

While they were debating what route to take, someone spotted and apparition of a horseman dressed in an antique military uniform from the Revolutionary War. Bathed in an unearthly glow, the horseman waved his tricorn hat at the men and urged them to follow him down one of the roads.

At first the soldiers thought the figure was a real person, General McClellan, returning to take command, but as the tired, yet excited soldiers followed the figure, another name circulated through their ranks.

By all accounts both officers and enlisted men were told that it was none other than George Washington leading them to Gettysburg.

Miraculous as this would seem, it wasn't the last the men of the 20th Maine would see of General George Washington. One of the most critical battles at Gettysburg was the Battle of Little Round Top. And as fate would have it, the men of the 20th Maine were right in the center of it.

According to history, when his men were running low on ammunition, Colonel Chamberlain ordered a bayonet charge. A risky strategy, but one that worked! The Confederates actually surrendered. So how did Colonel Chamberlain pull it off? Some people who were at Little Round Top that day claimed that as Chamberlain ordered the bayonet charge, the figure of George Washington appeared with a blazing sword and lead the charge on the terrified Alabamian Rebel soldiers.

Sounds a bit far fetched, right? Well, the government felt there must be something to the story, because Secretary of War Stanton dispatched a staff officer named Colonel Pittenger to investigate the account. After he questioned several eyewitnesses, his final report was never published and was supposed to be kept a secret from the general public.

Years later, when Colonel Chamberlain was a very old man, a reporter questioned him about the supernatural appearance of George Washington that fateful July day in 1863. Chamberlain thought for a while before giving the young man his answer. Then nodding his head, he said, "Yes, that report was circulated through our lines, and I have no doubt that it had a tremendous psychological effect in inspiring the men. Doubtless it was a superstition, but who among us can say that such a thing was impossible. We have not yet sounded or explored the immortal life that lies out beyond the Bar.

"We know not what mystic power may be possessed by those who are bivouacking with the dead. I only know the effect, but I do believe that we were enveloped by the powers of the otherworld that day and who shall say that Washington was not among the number of those who aided the country he founded?"

Section Three:

SPIRITS

OF THE

SOUTHERN

COLONIES

T he Provinces of Maryland, North and South Carolina, Georgia and the Colony and Dominion of Virginia, Kentucky, and West Virginia all make up what is known as the Southern Colonies of British America.

The Southern Colonies operated in a very different manner compared to the New England Colonies and the Middle Colonies. A different way of life was lived by the inhabitants of the south. Where the Northern Colonists, like the Quakers and the Puritans were coming to the colonies for religious freedom, the Southern Colonists were being drawn to America in search of gold, fresh farmland, and other riches that could be found there.

Even though the first plantations were originally worked by indentured servants as in the Northern Colonies, by the early eighteenth century the Southern landowners had all but replaced the indentured servants with slaves imported from Africa—something the Northern Colonies had never done. This is a change that would have huge social and political repercussions in the mid-nineteenth century and later be one of the main issues in the Civil War.

In the first three years of the Revolutionary War, the Southern colonies had barely seen much of the conflict. Most of the battles had been fought in the Northern Colonies, but after 1778, the Redcoats turned their attention to the South. Three years later, after having achieved some small victories, the British Army was weakening from the "hit and run" tactics of the Continental Army. The Siege of Yorktown, Virginia, finally broke them and British Commander Cornwallis surrendered in 1781. The fight for American independence may not have started in the South, but the Sons of Liberty triumphed there in the end.

The Southern Colonies have a multitude of paranormal and haunted locations. Starting with the very ghostly town of Annapolis, Maryland, to the tragic spirits of Robert Mackay's Trading Post in Georgia, you'll find that the spirit of southern hospitality is still alive…even in the afterlife.

9

The Province of Maryland

As a British Colony, Maryland has existed since 1632. In 1776, when the other thirteen original colonies declared independence from England, Maryland followed suit. Not only did they declare independence, but these residents of Maryland signed their names on the Declaration of Independence in 1776: Samuel Chase, William Paca, Thomas Stone and Charles Carroll.

For movie buffs, Charles Carroll was one of the keepers of the clues to the treasure in the movie *National Treasure*. Hollywood mythology aside, there are a few real life stories of hauntings in Maryland dating back to the Revolutionary War.

Even though no military battles were fought in Maryland, there were plenty of political moments with much heated emotion. Enough emotion to leave permanent psychic imprints on many old mansions and towns in Maryland, including the capital: Annapolis.

Old patriots still like to linger even now in some of their familiar haunts where the fate of the American Nation hung in the balance awaiting the outcome of choices they were forced to make.

From the many patriot spirits that reside in Annapolis, to the ghosts of some of the most famous founding fathers who still visit Montpelier Mansion, Maryland proves that it still stacks up to the rest of the original colonies as a home to some of history's most famous ghosts.

The Apparitions of Annapolis

Annapolis, the capital city of Maryland, dates back to 1649 when it was called Anne Arundel Town. Originally founded by Puritans who migrated from Virginia, they found the soil to be perfect for growing

The streets of Annapolis are literally filled with ghosts. *Courtesy of Cindy Wolf*

all kinds of crops and the small settlement flourished, becoming in 1694 the capitol and gaining its new name of Annapolis.

With a history as long as Annapolis has, you would think that there's at least a ghost story or two lurking about...and you'd be right!

The Library Ghost of the James Brice House

Close to the heart of the historic district of Annapolis, sits the "Most Haunted House in Annapolis." In a city that boasts of having no less than fourteen ghosts in their travel brochure, at least several of the most well known of them call the James Brice house their home.

Built in 1767, by James Brice, it's one of the largest colonial private homes of the Revolutionary War period. The Brice house takes up an impressive amount of space on East Street, right off of Prince George Street.

It was a fairly difficult task to actually get the whole house in view to take a picture with our digital camera. The monumental Georgian style home is just too massive to take a full front view picture, so I had to move across the street and take it on an angle.

The James Brice House, "the most haunted house in Annapolis." *Courtesy of Cindy Wolf*

The James Brice house is built like many other Georgian Mansions of the colonial period. It's very similar to Montpelier Mansion in Laurel, Maryland, and also to the William Paca Mansion on Prince George Street right around the corner. How the builders managed to squeeze a two and half story, fourteen-room mansion in that space is nothing short of incredible, and it didn't come cheap.

It took seven long years to build and cost over four thousand British pounds to create the mansion. A cost that in today's current price would cost over a million dollars.

James Brice hosted many guests in his house, as the Governor of Maryland in 1792 and as Mayor of Annapolis. Some of his more noteworthy guests included George and Martha Washington, Nathanael Greene, and the Marquee De Lafayette.

The house is reputed to have a number of hidden passages, and it is one of these secret areas that may harbor a ghost.

One of the most frequently sighted spirits is that of a young woman dressed in colonial-era style clothing. Her spirit always manifests just before dusk and has been seen floating from room to room as if in search of someone or something. She eventually glides silently over to the parlor room with a sad, discouraged look. She leans on the mantle by the fireplace and puts her face in her hands and begins to weep. Just as the lights start to come on she fades away... only to appear again on another night to start her fruitless search all over again and again.

In the 1940s some workmen who were repairing a wing of the house made a gruesome discovery. What they found was a closet sealed behind the plaster wall, and inside the secret closet they found a woman's skeleton. Perhaps it's this unfortunate soul who is the spirit that wanders throughout the house in the early evening hours. Rumor has it that the woman was a member of the Brice family who suffered from some form of mental illness. In order to avoid a scandal they kept her locked away in a secret room, and when she died, to avert an ugly legal and social embarrassment, they just hid her body in the room and sealed it with plaster.

The spirit of James Brice has also been encountered. During the 1920s, a professor from the Naval Academy was staying in the Brice House when it was used as faculty apartments for the Academy. He claims to have had several supernatural encounters in the house.

One night he was awoken from a sound sleep and saw the hazy, transparent figure of a man wearing a powdered wig and dressed in a plum-colored suit. He got the distinct impression that it was Colonel James Brice. The professor claims that this spirit walked right through the bed he was sleeping in and disappeared into thin air. After spending so much money and time on the house, it's only natural that Colonel Brice would want to check to see how it's been maintained over the centuries.

The house passed out of the Brice family in 1876, when James Brice's grandchildren sold it. The house has had several owners over the years and has been used as faculty apartments.

Since 1979, the Brice house has been owned by The International Union of Bricklayers and Allied Craftsmen who use it as a museum for the masonry arts. They open the house and give tours several times a year, usually during the Christmas season.

If you'd like to visit the Brice House, it's a fairly easy walk from the downtown Annapolis historic district. The best advice I can give you, is that if you plan on visiting Annapolis, park in the Navy stadium lot, where you can park all day for only $5.00 (at the writing of this book), and then take the free shuttle trolley into town. The day my wife and I visited Annapolis, they were having a street festival (something the city does every third Sunday of the month), so if you you're looking for a quiet time to go and get a glimpse of some Annapolis history, you'd be well advised to go on another day.

The Ghost in the Window

Just around the corner from the James Brice House is the sprawling William Paca House and Gardens. Located at 186 Prince George Street, the William Paca House takes up two acres of space and stands today as one of Annapolis' most elegant examples of Georgian architecture and colonial pleasure gardens.

The spirit of William Paca has been seen staring out one of these windows.
Courtesy of Cindy Wolf

William Paca, the original builder of the house, was one of the signers of the Declaration of Independence. While William Paca may not have fought as a soldier in the Revolutionary War, he put his political skills to good use and lead the way for the patriot movement to flourish and gain a foothold in Annapolis.

As the founding father of one of the local chapters of the "Sons of Liberty," he gained political and social popularity, which allowed him to be elected to more prominent positions in later years. William Paca argued in favor of separating Maryland from British rule and served time as a representative in Maryland's first and second Continental Congress. When it became time to vote for American independence, he wholly approved and traveled all the way to Philadelphia, Pennsylvania, in 1776 to sign the Declaration of Independence.

After the war, William Paca served as Governor of Maryland for three terms. When George Washington became president, he appointed Paca as a Federal District Court Judge. Paca held this post until his death in 1799. But, has William Paca moved on?

Some people think not. According to local Annapolis residents, a gentleman dressed in the colonial garb of a well-to-do landowner has been seen staring out of the upper windows of the William Paca house. This staring spirit bears a strong resemblance to the portrait of William Paca painted by Charles Wilson Peale in 1772. But William Paca isn't the only ghost in residence at the William Paca house.

Evidently haunting runs in the Paca family. William Paca's daughter's spirit has also been seen lounging about the grand staircase of the mansion. William Paca sold the house in 1780, and ever since it's had various owners and renters through the past few centuries.

In 1901, the house was turned into a hotel called, "Carvel Hall," and for the next sixty-four years, it reigned as one of Annapolis' most popular hotels. In 1965, however, the future of the William Paca house looked uncertain.

A real estate developer had plans to demolish the house and build an office and apartment complex on the spot. Fortunately, the Historic Annapolis Foundation, along with a privately funded,

Both William Paca and his daughter's spirit have been seen in this house and gardens. *Courtesy of Cindy Wolf*

If not for some civic and historic minded people, this house would've been demolished. *Courtesy of Cindy Wolf*

local preservationist managed to raise the money to acquire the property and restore it to its former glory. After years of research and restoration, including restoring the pleasure garden, the William Paca House opened its doors to the public for the first time, appropriately on exactly 200 years to the day when William Paca signed the Declaration of Independence.

The Middleton Tavern

In the heart of Annapolis' historic district, at 2 Market Place, sits one of Annapolis' oldest establishments. It's also one of the most haunted.

The Middleton Tavern was built during the Pre-Revolutionary days in the mid-1700s. It was purchased by a man named Horatio Middleton as an inn for seafaring men. During and after the Revolutionary War, many historic figures have stayed and dined at the Middleton Tavern. At any given time you might have seen the likes of George Washington, (Man, he really was everywhere!), Thomas Jefferson, and Ben Franklin, all dining at the there.

Hungry for both food and "spirits? You'll find both at the Middleton Tavern.
Courtesy of Cindy Wolf

During the Revolutionary War, the Middleton Tavern was operated by a man named George Mann, but after the war ended Samuel Middleton's son, Gilbert, took over the operation until 1870.

The Middleton Tavern was a very important stopping place during the war. Early travelers, including George Washington often stopped there while waiting to take the ferry across the Chesapeake Bay.

Jerry Hardesty is the current owner of the Middleton Tavern and has restored it both inside and out. He's also response able for changing the name of the building back to the Middleton Tavern from the name change made by the previous owners. In 1983, Hardesty started remodeling and expanding the building. As in most cases, if an old building goes through extensive remodeling, the paranormal energy seems to increase and there are many more instances of supernatural phenomena.

Here are some examples of just a few things that have happened over the years in the Middleton Tavern. On a regular basis both employees and customers have witnessed plates flying by themselves off of tables and glasses that sit on shelving around the bar area will suddenly fall off the shelves one-by-one as if some invisible entity is knocking them off in order.

An extreme example of poltergeist activity occurred when a table tipped over on its own, sending plates, silverware, and glasses crashing to the floor.

A tavern employee claims to have seen a man wearing colonial-style clothing staring out the window towards the harbor, as if waiting for a ship to dock. The employee watched in dismay as the man faded out of sight.

The Middleton Tavern is easy to find in the historic district of Annapolis, should you want to investigate it yourself. With all the paranormal activity there, and other places in Annapolis, you might just find yourself face-to-face with one of the many spirits in residence there.

The Manifestations of Montpelier Mansion

Montpelier Mansion is a national historic landmark located in Laurel, Maryland. It was built shortly after the Revolutionary War by Major Thomas Snowden and his wife, Anne Ridgeley Snowden. On the day Cindy and I decided to visit Montpelier Mansion, we were immediately impressed by the Georgian style architecture.

Welcome to Montpelier Mansion, host to some very famous historical ghosts.
Courtesy of Cindy Wolf

George and Martha Washington loved to visit this house. Some people claim they still do. *Courtesy of Cindy Wolf*

The sprawling mansion consists of a central blockhouse (which is the main part of the mansion) and two bullet-shaped wings connected by two small hallways called hyphens. The mansion is surrounded by lush parklands with trees like magnolia and holly, to name a few, and a formal picket fenced-in garden.

Major Snowden was considered a wealthy, well-connected businessman in his day. He was part-owner in his family's ironwork business. Ironwork was a very profitable business in those days. Snowden also owned 9,000 acres of land.

The Snowdens, as befitting their social standing in the community, held many lavish parties. Many of these parties were attended by some famous people such as George and Martha Washington, Thomas Jefferson, and John Adams. Strangely enough, it's not the spirits of the Snowden family that are reputed to haunt Montpelier, but rather some of its most famous visitors.

Montpelier was sold out of the Snowden family in 1890, and since that time, the mansion has had numerous owners over the years until 1961.

After the deaths of the owners, Mr. and Mrs. Breckenridge Long, the house was acquired by the Maryland National Capital Parks and Planning Commission who still own and operate it to this day.

On the day we visited the mansion, it was fortunate for us that they were having a special family program and the mansion was due to be open much later than normal that day. We were able to go on our own self-guided tour, because the last of the guided tours had stopped an hour before we arrived.

Since we were more interested in seeing if we could capture some paranormal activity, it suited us just fine not to have a guided tour. First we walked around outside the mansion taking pictures of the Georgian architecture.

After that, we entered the mansion through the garden terrace entrance, where a volunteer gave us a self-guided tour map of the mansion. Montpelier has been fully restored to its original colonial splendor and is filled with room upon room of antiques and reproduction furnishings to show what life would have been like in the house during the eighteenth century. Many of the original Snowden family antiques are on display in the exhibit case in the hyphen that leads to the dining room. Thanks to a household inventory list left by Thomas Snowden's son, Nicholas, the museum has been able to fairly reproduce how the rooms may have looked when the Snowdens occupied the house.

Could some of the original furnishings be the cause of the hauntings?
Courtesy of Cindy Wolf

Many times when a house has been restored or refurbished with long lost original artifacts, it can trigger what is known as a residual haunting. A residual or mindless haunting is kind of like the playback on a DVD player or a digital recorder. There's no thought behind it, because it's just replaying a scene from the past. Sometimes only certain people can pick-up the energy and witness the playback. Usually, these are people with a highly developed psychic ability. Perhaps this is what is occurring at Montpelier Mansion.

Many people over years have claimed to have witnessed apparitions of the likes of George Washington, Martha Washington, Thomas Jefferson, and John Adams. These spirits are said to walk the grounds of Montpelier.

As I've mentioned in my previous book, *Ghosts of Hershey and Vicinity*, sometimes spirits return from the afterlife because of the happy times they've experienced in a certain place. From what I've learned of Montpelier history it would certainly seem as though this is the case. Most of the visits the founding fathers made to Montpelier were for festive and hospitable reasons.

It's my opinion that what people have been experiencing at Montpelier Mansion is not an active haunting. People are just witnessing psychic playback of some great times in Montpelier's past. In any case, a visit to Montpelier is highly recommended. The estate and grounds are very interesting to see, not just on a paranormal standpoint, but if you like history and great scenery, you'll be very impressed.

10

The Colony and Dominion of Virginia, Kentucky, and W. Virginia

The Colony and Dominion of Virginia was one of the first colonies to start discussing the possibility of breaking away from British rule. As far back as 1763, the first talk of rebellion started being considered. The Virginia Legislature had a conflict over Clerical Salaries called the "Parson's Cause," with King George III. Future patriot Patrick Henry declared the king a tyrant.

Kentucky was originally a part of the Dominion of Virginia and was populated with mostly settlers from Virginia. During the 1750s, early explorers like Dr. Thomas Walker and Daniel Boone first settled the area. Kentucky had a volatile early history.

It was a major battleground during the Revolutionary War. The Native Americans that already resided there, the Shawnees, resented the settlers taking their land and allied themselves with the British during the war.

Life was so dangerous in Kentucky that a fort was built to protect the settlers from the attacks of the British and their Native American allies. One of the last battles of the Revolutionary War, The Battle of Blue Licks, was fought in Kentucky. The end of the war however didn't take place in Kentucky, but in Yorktown, Virginia.

In October of 1781, Lord Cornwallis, the General in charge of the British army, was forced to surrender at Yorktown, which essentially spelled the end to the Revolutionary War. Officially, the war ended with the signing of The Treaty of Paris in 1783.

The ending of the Revolutionary War hasn't stopped patriots from beyond the grave making their presence known throughout Virginia and Kentucky. A visit to Williamsburg or Yorktown will easily prove that old patriots never truly die.

Williamsburg, Virginia

> *"Williamsburg at the Revolution, was a town of beauty and of architectural significance; its major buildings were milestones in the history of American style, its Palace Garden perhaps the most beautiful in America*
>
> ~*Fiske Kimball*

Williamsburg was at one time the capital of Virginia. Although that title now rests on the city of Richmond, Colonial Williamsburg is definitely the tourist capital and it's also one of the most haunted locations in Virginia.

A visit to Colonial Williamsburg is like stepping back into the eighteenth century. For a paranormal investigator or just someone

A number of orbs outside a church in colonial Williamsburg, Virginia.
Courtesy of Cindy Wolf

with a passing interest in the unexplained, Williamsburg is a smorgasbord of opportunity to learn more about the supernatural, firsthand. Almost every street and house in Williamsburg has at least one phantom or ghost story attached to it.

The Tragic Case of Lady Ann Skipwith

One of the best known ghost stories in Williamsburg takes place at the George Wythe House. It involves a gentleman named Sir Peyton Skipwith and his young wife, Lady Ann.

The legend goes something like this: A young Scottish woman with a volatile temper, named Ann Miller was born near Petersburg, Virginia in 1741. At a very young age, she married Sir Peyton Skipwith and they settled down to live a comfortable and social life in Mecklenbury County.

Sir Peyton Skipwith was a wealthy, plantation owner, and he and Lady Ann would make several lengthy trips to Williamsburg and would stay there for weeks at a time. On one particular trip, on a summer evening, Lady Ann and Sir Peyton were invited to a gala social ball at the Governor's Palace. Since they were guests at the George Wythe House and it was only a short distance away, they chose to walk to the ball rather than take a carriage. They were dressed in their finest clothes. Lady Ann wore a new silk dress with matching red shoes and looked a vision of radiance.

After arriving and mingling with the other guests at the ball, for whatever reason, Lady Ann and Sir Peyton engaged in a heated argument, and Lady Ann tearfully, angrily, fled the party into the muggy, dark night. As she ran across the grassy sward that stretched between the Governor's Palace and the George Wythe house, she stumbled and fell onto the wet grass and lost one of her red shoes in the process. Even though the shoe was precious to her, she picked herself up and continue running, her eyes blurred from salty tears, she barged her way through the front door of the Wythe House and rushed up the main staircase.

She was truly a sight to behold as she staggered up the stairs, one shoe missing making a sound like a sailor with a peg leg walking the deck of a ship, as she clacked up the wooden stairs. She ran to her room just as the clock struck midnight, the witching hour! The line between fact and fiction gets blurry at this point of the story.

The legend claims that the reason Lady Ann fled the ball that night was because she thought that her husband, Sir Peyton was

These two pictures were taken a few seconds apart, outside the George Wythe House. *Courtesy of Cindy Wolf*

Take notice of the two orbs in the picture. Can you spot them? *Courtesy of Cindy Wolf*

having an affair with her sister, Jean. In true melodramatic style, Ann supposedly committed suicide that very night by throwing herself off the upstairs balcony of the Wythe House.

Over the centuries, employees and visitors to the George Wythe House have had many paranormal encounters. Are they because of Lady Ann? You be the judge. On the anniversary of the grand ball, the sound of someone running up the stairs with one shoe on and one off has been heard. Lady Ann's spirit has been observed exiting the closet in the room that used to be her bedroom wearing a fancy satin ball gown and red shoes. (She must've eventually found the lost one.)

Ann's apparition has also been seen sitting at her dressing table combing her hair. Truth be told, as entertaining as the legend is, the real story of Lady Ann Skipwith's death is rather mundane. She actually died in 1799 giving birth. Although she didn't die as suggested in the legend she definitely suffered a traumatic event here at Williamsburg and possibly her spirit has felt the need to return to the scene of her distress all those centuries ago.

Haunts in Yorktown

Between October 6th and 17th, the Continental Army laid siege to Yorktown, Virginia. When Lord Cornwallis had moved the British troops there and started to fortify the area, he had no idea that this was the worst move that he could possibly make during the Revolutionary War.

Thanks to the French reinforcements, the colonials managed to out-maneuver and out-gun the British. Cornwallis was cut off from the rest of the British army and had really no other choice than to surrender his troops to General George Washington, effectively ending the Revolutionary War.

Lord Cornwallis signed his surrender to Washington on October 19, 1781. In this small town of Yorktown, not more than a village really, it is this great event that has cast a ghostly history that dates all the way back to the Revolutionary War.

There are several haunted locations in Yorktown. One of them is the Nelson House, which is right on the main street. During the Revolutionary War, this house, built by Thomas Nelson, Jr., a signer of the Declaration of Independence, was Lord Cornwallis' headquarters.

Over the years, many people have had paranormal encounters with whatever entity resides here in the form of inexplicable rushes of cold air, and the sound of disembodied voices. Some people have also sighted the apparition of a British soldier on the first floor of the house. In the field across from the Nelson House, spirits dressed in red coats such as British soldiers would have worn, have been seen about the property, and it almost seems as if they're preparing for a battle. Witnesses have claimed to have seen them running across the field in military formation and then ducking behind trees for cover.

Other Revolutionary War era hauntings are also in Yorktown. Along the York River, there's a small cave nicknamed, "Cornwallis' Cave," due to a rumor that Lord Cornwallis hid here during the siege of Yorktown. Most historians think that it's unlikely that he would've sought refuge in a cave rather than his own headquarters when he was going to surrender. Why would he have needed to hide? Many of the civilian townspeople did, however briefly, use the cave as a refuge from the ensuing battle. Perhaps that's why, to this day, the sounds of screams and terrified hushed voices emanate from the cavern even though its empty.

11

The Province of North Carolina

North Carolina was named after King Charles I of England. The reason it's named Carolina and not Charlesania or Charlina is because his Latin name was Carolus. The first settlers in North Carolina were British colonists who had migrated from Virginia because of the dwindling amount of farmland that was available there.

As the Province of North Carolina grew and prospered, it was settled by two distinct cultures of immigrants. In eastern North Carolina, the influx of new settlers came from England and Scotland. In the western part of North Carolina, the settlers tended to be of Scots-Irish descent from Ireland and also from Germany.

This division of cultures had a huge effect on North Carolina during the Revolutionary War. The English and Scottish settlers in the eastern part of the province allied themselves with the crown and a majority of them became loyalist fighters or Tories during the war.

On the other hand the Scot-Irish of the western part of the province saw that being independent of the crown of England was more advantageous so they sided with the patriot cause.

On April 12, 1776, North Carolina's Continental Congress voted to succeed from the British rule and declared it's independence along with the other original thirteen colonies. From that point on, and throughout the years of the Revolution, North Carolina saw its fair share of fierce fighting.

Local militias of both Loyalists and Patriots went at each other with a vengeance. Thanks to an American victory at the battle of

King's Mountain, the Loyalists were dealt a severe setback. Because the majority of Tories involved in the battle were defeated, it prevented the Redcoats from gaining any more recruits among the Tories in the area; this severely weakening their fighting strength.

North Carolina also has a very haunted history. From the tragic events of the old Hammock House, to the haunted house in the horseshoe, the ghosts and specters that reside in the Province of North Carolina make their presence known to visitors even today 200 years later.

Hammock House's Bloody Stairs

Facing Beaufort Inlet on the coast of North Carolina at Cape Lookout, sits a huge, sturdy log building known as Hammock House. Since the early 1700s, this huge hall has been the highlight of many officers' social life.

Many years ago, a tragic mistake happened in this house and the bloody results have never been able to be washed away. They say it was a crime of passion and misunderstanding. But, what happened all those years ago to cause this now-deserted building to be plagued by blobs of supernatural glowing lights and the sounds of a desperate sword fight?

It started with Captain Madison Brothers, a quick-tempered man who was engaged to be married. He was returning to Hammock House to meet his fiancée after his recent voyage. Captain Brothers' ship arrived early in port and he thought he'd surprise his fiancée. It turns out he'd be getting the surprise, and an unwelcome one at that.

As he entered the stairway, he saw his fiancée kissing and embracing another man! Enraged beyond rational thought at his betrayal, Captain Brothers ran up the staircase, barging through the crowd of people on the stairs, and plunged his sword through the man's chest without waiting to hear any explanations of his actions. His aim was true and he stabbed the man right through the heart, killing him instantly! After committing the horrible deed, the fog of anger lifted from Captain Brothers and he caught just a glimpse of his terrified bride to be running away from him in terror.

Later he found out that the man he had murdered wasn't his fiancée's secret lover, but her brother, a seaman named Carruthers Ashley, of whom she hadn't seen in several years. Ever since that fateful and tragic day, whenever there's a fog or a particularly humid day, the bloodstains belonging to the unfortunate Carruthers Ashley that cover the stairs turn a darker shade of red and become more prominent on the upper staircase.

Just like the bloody hearthstone in "The Canterville Ghost," no amount of scrubbing has ever been able to wash those guilty stains away.

The Haunted House in the Horseshoe

In 1781, a small battle took place between British troops and the owner of the Alston House, Colonel Philip Alston. The resulting outcome of the battle was the arrest of Colonel Alston, but he was released on parole later, much as many officers were in those days. Even so, scandal seemed to follow the Colonel the rest of his life.

Later in life he was implicated in a murder to which his response was awfully guilty looking. He left the area quickly before he was arrested. Over the years, the Alston House, which has also been called, "The House in the Horseshoe," because it was built near the sharp bend of the Deep River, is also reputed to be one of the most actively haunted houses in central North Carolina.

For years, people have been witnessing a strange light that emanates from the house grounds and then rises up into the air. In addition to the strange light, there is a high pitched vibration sound that echoes throughout the house, and often people hear a disembodied voice whispering in the fireplace. Is it the ghost of Colonel Alston? Most people who have investigated the house believe it is.

12

The Province of South Carolina

T he Province of South Carolina had its start the same way North Carolina did, with King Charles II giving the land that would be both North and South Carolina to a group of eight noblemen called the Lord Proprietors.

Until the early 1700s, both North and South Carolina were governed by the noblemen, but in 1719, the British crown bought back the land of South Carolina colony and started appointing a royal governor.

Just as in North Carolina, there were two types of cultural immigrants to South Carolina. In a complete reversal of North Carolina, the Scot-Irish settlers took the Loyalist side of the Revolutionary War and became Tories, unlike their counterparts in North Carolina that were pro-American. The English and French colonists on the other hand took the side of the Patriots where in North Carolina their fellow Englishmen actually fought for the crown during the war.

From the Battle of Blackstock Farm to the Wedgefield Plantation, there are several Revolutionary War haunts just begging to be investigated.

The Black Dog of Blackstock Battlefield

The battle of Blackstock's Farm took place in Union County, South Carolina, on November 20, 1780. It really had its start a month earlier due to the crushing defeat of the British forces at King's Mountain in North Carolina.

Cornwallis, general and commander of the British army in the colonies was upset that these American upstarts, the Patriots, had defeated and or captured not less than 900 Redcoats at the Battle of King's Mountain. He was frustrated by the fact that these backwater settlers, hardly even trained in combat, could've beaten his highly trained army and wanted to teach them a lesson in humility, not to mention to restore his reputation as a leader.

To accomplish this he required none but the best of his officers. Cornwallis ordered his most gifted officer, a man named Lieutenant Colonel Banastre Tarlton, who had never lost a battle, to disrupt the actions of the patriot militia operating in the Carolinas. It was a force that was growing in power and he wanted to put an end to their rampages.

Colonel Tarlton was perhaps the most hated and feared man in the Carolinas and he set his sights on attacking General Thomas Sumter's militia, defeating him and regaining the trust of the Loyalist living in the South Carolina.

But what Lieutenant Colonel Tarlton didn't know was that the Patriots, under the supervision of General Sumter, had been steadily gaining volunteers and were about a thousand men strong in force. A few days before the actual battle at Blackstock's Farm, on November 18th, Tarlton and his regiment, the 63rd, were resting their horses on the Broad River.

Seizing the opportunity to harass them with some guerrilla warfare, a raiding party of patriot militia decided to take some potshots at them from the opposite bank of the river. Given the circumstances, if perhaps another officer other than Tarlton had been in command of the British, they might've just shrugged off the attack and moved on with their mission. Not so with Tarlton.

Tarlton was not a man who would easily turn away from an insult, and that's exactly what he felt the Americans who fired on his troops had done. He took it as a person insult. That very night he forced his men to cross the river using flatboats so that they could pursue the patriot militia who had fired on them earlier in the day. Maybe if Tarlton had not been such a hard commander, one of his own troopers wouldn't have felt the need to desert and go over to the enemy.

The 63rd regiment deserter revealed to Thomas Sumter, Tarlton's attack plans and his very location. General Sumter, being no fool, did not hesitate to take advantage of this vital information. Summoning his colonels, General Sumter planned a strategy to defeat the undefeated Colonel Tarlton. Sumter's plan was based on the idea of Colonel Thomas Braden. Braden was a local man who was very familiar with the backwoods area. He suggested they take positions on the farm of William Blackstock. In his opinion, the land was perfectly suited to their needs. It had already been cleared out and would provide an excellent field of fire. Plus, there were several sturdy, log outbuildings to provide cover for flanking the enemy, but the most advantageous terrain feature of all was the dense woods that surrounded the farm on higher ground. They felt it would provide excellent cover for the militia riflemen.

As predicted, Colonel Tarlton approached the awaiting patriots late in the afternoon of November 20th. In a very reckless, but typical for him, move, Tarlton ordered a full frontal assault. It was foolish on his part because he knew that his troops were outnumbered by the Patriots, but his sense of pride had been hurt and he was arrogant enough to believe that these rag-tag Rebels were no match for his highly trained British soldiers.

The attack went badly in the beginning for the continental militia. The Patriots made the mistake of firing too soon and misjudging the distance from the British attackers. This gave the Redcoats a chance to advance and to take little damage from the first barrage of musket fire. The Patriots didn't have enough time to reload before the British were on top of them brandishing their bayonets. Unfortunately, for the British, this is where they made their first mistake. The 63rd Regiment, in their haste to confront the Patriot militia, had advanced too far beyond their own lines and were cut off from the rest of the troops. They were also too close to the outbuilding where waiting in the wings more Patriot riflemen were able to fire on the hapless Redcoats.

As a result, a major and two lieutenants were killed and at least one third of the privates in the regiment were killed or wounded as well. The Americans on the other hand only suffered very minor losses, perhaps a couple of men wounded at most. In addition to getting a chance to pick off a few British officers, the Patriots managed to pull a flanking maneuver around them effectively cutting them off and allowing the Continental Army to attack the Calvary Dragoons that had not yet even entered the battle from the rear of the British lines.

By this time you might have thought that Colonel Tarlton could see that it was time to retreat and cut his losses. But Tarlton, more concerned with his undefeated reputation than for his outnumbered troops, hastily issued the order for his Cavalry Dragoons to charge in the open, up the hill, towards the Patriots who were still hidden in the cover of the woods.

The charge was short and fierce. The score was, Patriots: 1, Dragoons: 0. According to written reports of the battle, there were so many wounded horses and riders that the road to the woods was blocked by the wounded and dying men and horses.

Finally Tarlton saw how the cards were falling and despite the black mark on his reputation called for an orderly retreat to his commanders and had to leave at least fifty wounded and dead soldiers on the battlefield.

General Sumter put aside what common sense he had and decided to go closer to the retreating British to watch them leave. In doing so, he opened himself up to attack as the retreating 63rd regiment opened fire on Sumter and his officers.

Sumter was critically wounded and had to relinquish command. In the end, Tarlton was defeated, but not gone entirely from the battle. The next morning he'd planned to regroup his regiment and go back to re-attack the militia, but they were already long gone. Left holding the proverbial bag, Colonel Tarlton was forced to make his troops bury the wounded on both sides and to tend to their wounded men.

To save face with his commanding officer, Colonel Tarlton actually lied in his report to Lord Cornwallis, telling him that he had routed the Patriot militia and over exaggerating the wounds to General Sumter, and played down his humiliating retreat.

Today, the Blackstock farmhouse battlefield is part of a national park in Union, South Carolina. The passage of time has changed this area very little and it still looks very much the same as it did when the battle raged there on that day in November of 1780.

Over the years, visitors to the battlefield park have reported hearing the phantom sounds of battle. Sounds such as muskets being fired, troops marching, and a full blown cavalry charge have been heard at various times.

People have also heard the screams and moans of men dying. All of these disembodied sounds could possibly be the psychic imprint of that battle. Psychic recording of other battles have been reported all over the world and from many different time periods. Because of the remoteness of the battlefield, not as many tourists visit here as they would, for example, Valley Forge in Pennsylvania or Yorktown in Virginia, so not as many paranormal encounters have been recorded happening over the years here as in those locations. That doesn't mean they haven't happened though.

A reoccurring sighting of a large phantom black dog that appears out of nowhere and follows visitors around is the most often reputed paranormal phenomenon. According to eyewitnesses, the dog materializes near the woods and will follow visitors and their cars as they exit the battlefield and then disappear into thin air.

This phantom hound has been known to appear and then disappear only to reappear a great distance away from where it was first spotted only a few minutes prior. By the most recent accounts this phantom black dog is still making appearance to this day.

Which brings us to the interesting question of: Why does this spectral dog appear? Chances are, if it's anything like the phantom black dog in England known as a Barghest or Black Shuck it's an omen of doom.

Usually, in the folktales involving a ghostly black hound, whoever sees one typically dies within a year of the sighting.

Supposedly, the paranormal hounds are drawn to desolate places. They are sometimes drawn to places where a great and fatal tragedy happened in the past. In the case of the Blackstock Battlefield, perhaps the phantom black dog was lured there during the battle in 1780 and hasn't left.

The Ghost of Georgetown

Georgetown, South Carolina, is on the northeast coast. When the Revolutionary War broke out, Georgetown contributed two signers of the Declaration of Independence: Thomas Lynch, Sr. and Thomas Lynch, Jr. During the war, the Marquee De Lafayette arrived in Georgetown to help fight the British. Georgetown was very important to the Continental Army during the war as a port city. As a supply port, Georgetown helped General Nathanael Greene's army.

Wedgefield Plantation

Wedgefield Plantation is a modern day resort community five miles north of Georgetown. The community may be modern, but its history, both mundane and supernatural, goes far back into South Carolina ancestry. Wedgefield was one of the first land grants in Province of South Carolina.

There was once more than one manor house at Wedgefield. The oldest and smaller one was built in the early 1760s, and another, larger one was built much later. The one our paranormal interest lies in is the first one. This Revolutionary War era building is haunted by the ghost of a headless British soldier.

The gruesome story of how this British sentry lost his life...and his head...goes something like this: The owner of the Wedgefield

Plantation chose not to take sides when the Revolutionary War broke out. He felt the safest course of action was to remain neutral in the conflict. Besides, he had a personal interest in the British control of the colonies. His business depended on income from England. Even though he didn't outright support the Patriots, he had several family members who were actively involved in the cause of liberty.

At some point during the war, some patriotic American soldiers were being held prisoner at the Wedgefield Plantation. The owner's daughter was secretly working with a scout for the legendary American freedom fighter, Francis Marion, A.K.A. The Swamp Fox.

The owner's daughter and her ally, the scout, soon came up with a daring, yet cunning, plan to free the American prisoners. The plan was simple. The owner's daughter contrived a visit to the nearby Mansfield Plantation. Since these were dangerous times and known Rebels were reported to be in the area, she easily persuaded her father to allow all but one of the British soldiers guarding the prisoners to escort her on her journey to the Mansfield Plantation.

The very next day, as was agreed, all the guards but one accompanied the owner's daughter on her trip. All was going according to plan. The scout had informed Francis Marion that the rescue attempt was on schedule.

Just as it was turning twilight, a group of Francis Marion's soldiers, led by the Swamp Fox himself, galloped their horses up the road to Wedgefield Plantation. The deepening night's shadows concealed their true identity.

Horses make a lot of noise at galloping speed and the sound of many horses galloping is very hard to conceal. The lone British sentry, left his post of guarding the prisoners, heard their approach as plain as day, and assumed that the riding party was a another group of his own comrades coming from the nearby Georgetown. He never suspected that they were Rebels coming to free the prisoners.

The Rebels seized the opportunity of surprise as the sentry ran down the steps to greet them. Only then at close range did he realize his fatal mistake. He tried to fire his pistol, but only got off one shot that went wild and hit nothing. At the same precise moment, Francis Marion, the Swamp Fox, welding a razor sharp cavalry saber, severed the man's head from his shoulders in one clean sweep.

According to the other men who were there that night, the gruesome scene happened so fast, that the headless body actually convulsed and staggered for a few seconds like a chicken that had just been beheaded before it eventually fell to the ground lifeless and spewing copious amounts of blood.

The vision must've been truly horrifying to see, because as long as they lived, the men would always tell the tale they'd seen to anyone who asked.

The Swamp Fox and his men quickly rescued the American prisoners and took them back to his hidden encampment.

As for the ill-fated British sentry, his body (and I presume his head) was buried in the garden near the original Wedgefield Manor. Only seven weeks after his body was buried, the gruesome headless specter of the British guard was spotted staggering around the garden, waving a pistol, presumably searching for his missing head.

Over the last few centuries, people living nearby have seen this unfortunate soul. Not only has he been seen in the garden, but some people claim that very late on moonlit nights, you can see the ghost pacing back and forth on the porch as if he were still performing his old sentry duty. Evidently, he must have found his head, because when he's on the porch, he's not headless.

At other times, strange noises prelude the spirit's appearance in the garden. Sometimes, people will hear the sound of many galloping horses and other times it sounds as though heavy chains are being dragged somewhere.

In any case, when the spirit makes his headless grotesque appearance, he doesn't fail to frighten anyone who gets a good look at him. In the 1930s, the old Wedgefield House was demolished, but the current manor, while not colonial in origin is still a fine architectural showpiece, complete with an expansive garden.

The headless Redcoat doesn't make as many appearances as he once did when the old house was still there, but many times odd noises will be heard in the new manor house. Since it's right near the spot of his eternal resting place, perhaps the ghostly sentry has taken up a new guard post in the house.

13

The Province of Georgia

Massive settlements of the English in Georgia started in the early 1730s. Despite the popular belief that it was set up as a penal colony for debtors and criminals from England, it was never meant to be used as such a place. Granted, a large number of colonists were sent their from the overcrowded prisons, that wasn't the main reason the colony was chartered – although that's the big historical misconception.

In 1752, Georgia became a royal colony, and by this time, most of the original, poorer settlers were being replaced with wealthy immigrants migrating from South Carolina. Georgia never did declare its independence from England like the other colonies, but they did adopt a State Constitution in 1776.

While there were many patriots living and operating against the crown during the Revolutionary War, there were also a large number of Loyalists still in control of the governments in Georgia. Near the end of the Revolution, Georgia was one of the few places left with a functioning Loyalist government still intact.

The Thirteen Ghosts of Mackay's Trading House

Robert Mackay's Trading Post is a three-story wooden structure that was used as a colonial trading post. It is also considered to be one of America's most haunted houses due to the executions that took place here early in the Revolutionary War.

The White House is another name for the Trading Post, and it was in this White House where very red blood was spilled in the name of freedom and liberty. Robert Mackay's Trading Post was

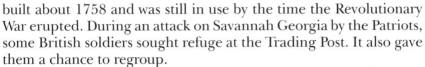

built about 1758 and was still in use by the time the Revolutionary War erupted. During an attack on Savannah Georgia by the Patriots, some British soldiers sought refuge at the Trading Post. It also gave them a chance to regroup.

With a stronger force, the Patriots laid siege to the Trading Post, trapping the British inside. The Patriots in turn were captured when British reinforcements from Fort Ninety-Six, from South Carolina arrived on the scene and surrounded them. Thirteen American Patriots (one for each of the rebelling colonies), were to be executed as an example.

Colonel Thomas Browne had each of the thirteen Rebels lined up on the staircase outside the front of the Trading Post. He then had nooses placed around their necks and had them hung all at the same time.

In addition to the patriots that were hung, he turned over another sixteen Patriots to his allies, the local Indian tribe, and allowed the Native Americans to exact revenge on them by torturing them to death in front of the Trading Post.

Today, Mackay's Trading Post still exists and is now operated by The Georgia Historical Commission and is open to the public for tours. Supposedly, the spirits of those Patriots who were executed still reside there.

An urban legend has it that if you stand on the staircase where the thirteen prisoners were executed and count to thirteen, you'll hear the sound of the nooses snapping their necks and the thuds of their bodies being hung. On the thirteenth step of the staircase, some people who have visited the building say you can hear the moans and groans of the Patriots who were tortured by the Indians.

Ghost Tours

If reading about Revolutionary War hauntings aren't enough to satisfy your curiosity about the supernatural, you might want to see some of these places for yourself. A good way to do this is to take a local ghost tour.

Here is a list I've compiled of ghost tours that are in some of the places I've written about in this book. This is by no means a complete list, just a sampling of what's out there.

When possible, I've included contact information, including a phone number and website for further information. As of this printing, all contact information is up to date.

Niagara On-The-Lake Ghost Walk
Niagara On-The-Lake, Canada
PHONE: (905) 529-4327
WEBSITE: www.hauntedhamilton.com

New England Curiosities Walking Tour
Portsmouth, NH
PHONE: (207) 439-8905
EMAIL: roxie@newenglandcuriosities.com

New England Ghost Tours
PHONE: (781) 235-7149
WEBSITE: www.newenglandghosttours.com

Salem Night Tour/Ghost Tour
Salem, MA
PHONE: (978) 741-1170
WEBSITE: www.salemghosttours.com

Providence Ghost Tour
Providence, RI
WEBSITE: www.providenceghosttour.com

Ghost of New York
New York, NY
PHONE: (718) 591-4741 or (888) NY-WALKO
EMAIL: drphil@newyorktalksandwalks.com

Ghost Tour of Philadelphia
Philadelphia, PA
PHONE: (215) 413-1997
WEBSITE: www.ghosttour.com/philadephia.html

Annapolis Ghost Tours
Annapolis, MD
PHONE: (800) 979-3370 or (212) 209-3370
WEBSITE: www.ghostsofannapolis.com

Candlelight Ghost Tours of Frederick
Frederick, MD
PHONE: (301) 668-8922
WEBSITE: www.marylandghosttours.com

Ghost Tour-Ocean City, NJ
Ocean City, NJ
PHONE: (609)-814-0199 or (610) 587-8303
WEBSITE: www.ghosttour.com/oceancity.html

Williamsburg Ghost-Lantern Tours
Williamsburg, VA
PHONE: (757) 897-9600
WEBSITE: www.williamsburgprivatetours.com

Asheville Haunted Ghost Tour
Asheville, NC
PHONE: (800) 920-7375
WEBSITE: www.northcarolinatours.net

Charleston Ghost and Dungeon Walking Tour
Charleston, SC
WEBSITE: www.charlestondungeon.com

The Ghosts and Legends of Savannah Walking Tour
Savannah, GA
PHONE: (877) 703-9225
WEBSITE: www.theghostsofsavannah.com

Bibliography

BOOKS

Adams III, Charles J. *Ghost Stories of Berks County.* Exeter House Books, Reading, PA, 1982.

Adams III, Charles J. *Bucks County Ghost Stories.* Exeter House Books, Reading, PA, 1999.

Adams III, Charles J. and Clothier, Gary Lee S. *Ghost Stories of Berks County Book 3.* Exeter House Books, Reading, PA, 1988.

Adams III, Charles J. *Philadelphia Ghost Stories.* Exeter House Books, Reading, PA, 1998.

Adams III, Charles J. *Pennsylvania Dutch Country Ghosts Legends and Lore.* Exeter House Books, Reading, PA, 1994.

Adams III, Charles J. *New York City Ghost Stories.* Exeter House Books, Reading, PA, 1996

Adams III, Charles J. and Seibold, David J. *Ghost Stories of the Lehigh Valley.* Exeter House Books, Reading, PA, 1993.

Adams III, Charles J. *Montgomery County Ghost Stories.* Exeter House Books, Reading, PA, 2000.

Adams III, Charles J. *Ghost Stories of Chester County and The Brandywine Valley.* Exeter House Books, Reading, PA, 2001.

Belanger, Jeff. *Encyclopedia of Haunted Places.* New Page Books, Franklin Lakes, NJ, 2005.

Bingham, Joan and Riccio, Delores. *More Haunted Houses.* Pocket Books, New Orkney, 1991.

Coleman, Christopher K. *Ghosts and Haunts of the Civil War.* Rutledge Hill Press, Nashville, TN, 1999.

DK Eyewitness Travel New England, St. Remy Media Inc., Montreal, Canada, 2007.

Forest, Christopher, *Boston's Haunted History.* Schiffer Publishing, LTD., Atglen, PA, 2008.

Guiley, Rosemary Ellen. *The Encyclopedia of Ghosts and Spirits.* Facts On File, Inc., New York, NY, 1992

Hauck, Dennis William. *Haunted Places, The National Directory.* Penguin Books, New York, NY, 1996.

Hoffman, Elizabeth P. *In Search of Ghosts.* Camino Books, Inc., Philadelphia, PA, 1992.

Holzer, Hans. *Where the Ghosts are: Favorite Haunted Houses in America and the British Isles.* Parker Publishing Company, Inc., West Nyack, NY, 1984.

Jarvis, Sharon. *Dead Zones.* Warner Books, Inc., New York, NY, 1992.

Kocher, A. Lawrence, and Dearstyne, Howard. *Colonial Williamsburg, It's Buildings and Gardens.* Colonial Williamsburg Inc., Williamsburg, VA, 1949.

Lake, Matt. *Weird Pennsylvania.* Sterling Publishing Co. Inc., New York, NY, 2005.

Norman, Michael and Scott, Beth. *Haunted America.* Tom Doherty Associates, Inc., New York, NY, 1994.

Roberts, Nancy. *Civil War Ghost Stories and Legends.* University of South Carolina Press, Columbia, SC, 1992.

Rovin, Jeff. *The Spirits of America.* Pocket Books, New York, NY, 1990.

Rowell, Melissa and Lynwander, Amy. *Baltimore's Harbor Haunts.* Schiffer Publishing, Atglen, PA, 2005.

Sarles Jr., Frank B., and Shedd, Charles E. *Colonials and Patriots.* United States Dept. of the Interior, National Park Service, Washington, DC, 1964.

Siebold, David J. and Adams III, Charles J. *Cape May Ghost Stories.* Exeter House Books, Barnegat Light, NJ, and Reading, PA, 1988.

Sieibold, David J., and Adams III, Charles J. *Pocono Ghosts, Legends and Lore.* Exeter House books, Reading, PA, 1991.

Tales of the Old Dutch Burying Ground/A Walking Tour. The Friends of the Old Dutch Burying Ground Inc., Sleepy Hollow, NY, 2001.

Tassin, Susan Hutchison. *Pennsylvania Ghost Towns.* Stackpole Books, Mechanicsburg, PA, 2007.

Toney, B. Keith. *Battlefield Ghosts.* Thomas Publications, Gettysburg, PA, 2008.

Winer, Richard and Osborn, Nancy. *Haunted Houses.* Bantam Books, New York, NY, 1979.

PERIODICALS

Brandywine Battlefield Pamphlet, Pennsylvania Historical and Museum Commission, 2008.

John Dickinson Mansion and Plantation Pamphlet, Delaware Historical and Cultural Affairs, Dover, DE.

Montpelier Mansion Self-Guided Tour Pamphlet, Prince George's County, Natural and Historic Resources Division, Laurel, MD, 2008

Rickenbach, Joel. "Eerie PA, Issue 1." Eerie PA, West Chester, PA, 2005.

"Valley Forge/Visitors Guide to Valley Forge Area and Montgomery County, PA." 2009

Valley Forge National Historical Park Pamphlet, National Park Service, U.S. Dept. of the Interior, 2009

WEBSITES

http://en.wikipedia.org/wiki/Jonathan_moulton
http://files.usgwarchives.org
http://hscc.carr.org/property/cockeys.htm
http://livinghistory.co.uk/1700-1800/articles/xw_121.html
http://portal.delaware.gov/facts/history/delhist.shtml
www.americanfolklore.net/folktales/pa2.html
www.charlestown-nh.gov
www.fortat4.org/history.php
www.geocities.com/varda_valar/genw/werefox.htm
www.hampton.lib.nh.us/hampton/blog/moultondaman.htm
www.hauntsandhistory.com
www.liberty1.org/gwvision.htm
www.seacoastnh.com
www.shadowlands.net
www.ushistory.org/valleyforge
www.wikipedia.org

Places Index

Courtesy of Cindy Wolf